Serious and
Unstable Condition

SERIOUS AND UNSTABLE CONDITION

Financing America's Health Care

Henry J. Aaron

THE BROOKINGS INSTITUTION
Washington, D.C.

Library of Congress Cataloging-in-Publication data:

Aaron, Henry J.
  Serious and unstable condition: financing America's health care / Henry
J. Aaron.
     p.   cm.
  Includes bibliographical references and index.
  ISBN 0-8157-0051-2 (alk. paper)—ISBN 0-8157-0050-4
(pbk: alk. paper)
  1. Medical economics—United States.   I. Title.
RA410.53.A27   1991
338.4'33621'0973—dc20   91-18516
                                                                    CIP

9 8 7 6 5 4 3 2

The paper used in this publication meets the minimum
requirements of the American National Standard for
Information Sciences—Permanence of Paper for Printed
Library Materials, ANSI Z39.48–1984.

⨐ THE BROOKINGS INSTITUTION

The Brookings Institution is an independent organization devoted to nonpartisan research, education, and publication in economics, government, foreign policy, and the social sciences generally. Its principal purposes are to aid in the development of sound public policies and to promote public understanding of issues of national importance.

The Institution was founded on December 8, 1927, to merge the activities of the Institute for Government Research, founded in 1916, the Institute of Economics, founded in 1922, and the Robert Brookings Graduate School of Economics and Government, founded in 1924.

The Board of Trustees is responsible for the general administration of the Institution, while the immediate direction of the policies, program, and staff is vested in the President, assisted by an advisory committee of the officers and staff. The by-laws of the Institution state: "It is the function of the Trustees to make possible the conduct of scientific research, and publication, under the most favorable conditions, and to safeguard the independence of the research staff in the pursuit of their studies and in the publication of the results of such studies. It is not a part of their function to determine, control, or influence the conduct of particular investigations or the conclusions reached."

The President bears final responsibility for the decision to publish a manuscript as a Brookings book. In reaching his judgment on the competence, accuracy, and objectivity of each study, the President is advised by the director of the appropriate research program and weighs the views of a panel of expert outside readers who report to him in confidence on the quality of the work. Publication of a work signifies that it is deemed a competent treatment worthy of public consideration but does not imply endorsement of conclusions or recommendations.

The Institution maintains its position of neutrality on issues of public policy in order to safeguard the intellectual freedom of the staff. Hence interpretations or conclusions in Brookings publications should be understood to be solely those of the authors and should not be attributed to the Institution, to its trustees, officers, or other staff members, or to the organizations that support its research.

To my daughter Lissa

Foreword

THE U.S. SYSTEM of financing health care faces three major problems: high and rising costs, no health insurance for millions of Americans and inadequate insurance for many more, and a lack of evaluation of many common medical procedures. It is a tired cliché to say that this system is in crisis, but it is also an undeniable fact. Reform of health care financing has emerged as a critical social policy issue of the decade.

Serious and Unstable Condition: Financing America's Health Care is a lay reader's guide to the emerging debate on how to reform the health care financing system. Henry J. Aaron reviews the problems confronting the government, private insurers, business, labor, physicians, hospital administrators, and the general population. He explains why health care is different from most other economic goods and how these differences should shape the choice among potential reforms. He sketches the basic facts needed to understand the U.S. system and describes relevant characteristics of other countries' arrangements. After outlining various proposals for reform, he presents a plan of his own.

Aaron is director of the Brookings Economic Studies program. He wishes to thank Robert M. Ball, Rashi Fein, Philip R. Lee, Jack A. Meyer, Joseph P. Newhouse, Robert D. Reischauer, and an anonymous referee for carefully reviewing and criticizing drafts of the manuscript. He also wishes to acknowledge an intellectual debt to

William B. Schwartz of Tufts University, whose insights and experience with the U.S. health care system influenced many aspects of this book. The author is grateful to Karan Singh for research assistance and to Kathleen Elliott Yinug for word processing assistance. Nancy D. Davidson edited the manuscript, Karan Singh and Pamela Plehn checked it for accuracy, Susan L. Woollen prepared it for typesetting, and Mary Kidd prepared the index.

Brookings gratefully acknowledges financial support from the Robert Wood Johnson Foundation.

The views expressed here are the author's alone and should not be ascribed to the persons whose assistance is acknowledged above or to the trustees, officers, and other staff members of the Brookings Institution.

BRUCE K. MACLAURY
President

April 1991
Washington, D.C.

Contents

Tables

Figures

Serious and
Unstable Condition

CHAPTER ONE

What Is the Problem?

THE HEALTH CARE system of the United States is marked by inconsistency and paradox. Americans like their doctors and report favorably on their latest contacts with the health care system. Yet they complain that the system is a mess and must be radically changed. Foreigners criticize the U.S. system for spending so much more than their own systems while leaving so many people uninsured. But they continue to come to the United States to receive sophisticated medical care and to study innovative ways of financing and delivering care. U.S. businesses allege that high and sharply rising costs of medical care hinder them in competition with companies in countries with national health plans, but most continue to cherish the decentralized U.S. system. Medical science generates a cornucopia of impressive new diagnostic and therapeutic procedures even as the federal government initiates studies to measure the efficacy of standard medical interventions, most of which have never been scientifically evaluated.

Three major problems confront the U.S. health care system in the 1990s. First, the cost of health care is higher and rising faster than in any other nation, and it is absorbing a rapidly growing share of national output. These trends defy repeated and remarkably unsuccessful efforts by corporations, unions, and the government to slow spending growth.

Second, roughly one nonelderly American in seven lacks any

1

insurance for the costs of health care for acute illnesses, and many have insurance that is seriously inadequate. Few are insured against the costs of long-term care, a major risk for the rapidly rising numbers of the very elderly and a minor risk for people of all ages. Much acute-care insurance incompletely protects beneficiaries against the cost of serious illness or particular risks. And many who are now insured will lose coverage as employers stop sponsoring insurance. Some employees will abandon coverage as employers shift costs to them.

Third, despite the unprecedented breadth and pace of advance in the science and technology of medical care, no solid scientific basis exists for many medical services. Some services are demonstrably overused and some underused, but few have been subject to rigorous evaluation.

None of these inconsistencies or paradoxes is new. Until recently, none was sufficiently severe to persuade any of the major stakeholders, or groups with an important interest in health care financing arrangements, that the system required major change. But the appeal of the current system to every one of these stakeholders is diminishing. A major theme of this book is that current arrangements for financing health care cannot endure. Clearly visible trends ensure the continuing erosion of support for the current financing system. Unless financing policy changes dramatically, the number of uninsured and spending on health care will both continue to grow. As a result, the national debate on the reform of health care financing that has already begun will lead to major legislation before the end of the decade.

Diminishing Support for the Current System

No major change in arrangements for health care financing has been made since the enactment of medicare and medicaid in 1965 because until recently every major group concerned with health care financing was doing quite well under the existing system. Business, organized labor, physicians, hospital administrators, suppliers of pharmaceuticals and medical equipment, insurance companies, and the insured all were more or less satisfied with the status quo. Although different modifications might have helped each of these groups, no major reform commanded the support of a politically effective majority.

During the 1970s employer-sponsored health insurance, the system serving most Americans, appealed to both business and labor. For business, health insurance was a fringe benefit of modest cost. Employers controlled the extent and structure of benefits. For organized labor, health insurance was a fringe benefit for which their leaders had fought. They could legitimately claim that through their efforts union members enjoyed especially generous benefits and increased economic security. Workers could buy insurance independently, but only at considerably greater cost because as individuals they would lose the tax advantages of employer-sponsored plans and the discounts provided to groups. Moreover, insurance costs were low enough and productivity growth fast enough to support both rising wages and improved health benefits.

For U.S. physicians, the system for financing health care was close to ideal. Upon emerging from the best medical schools in the world, trained to use the latest and most costly equipment, drugs, and medical techniques, they confronted a system of payment that gave them clinical freedom and rewarded them handsomely for doing exactly what they had been trained to do. Hospital managers were nearly equally blessed. The governmentally imposed regulatory restraints they faced were not very effective. In practice, hospital administrators could equip and maintain highly modern facilities and equipment, and the financing system enabled them to recover all of the costs of these purchases. Suppliers of medical equipment, devices, supplies, and pharmaceuticals had a corresponding capacity to sell to deep-pocketed customers who were willing to buy new products, regardless of whether improvements in quality were large or small relative to cost.

Insurance companies knew that they faced business purchasers interested in extending the range of coverage and willing to pay the costs to ensure rapid processing of claims. Moreover, buyers' cost consciousness was sufficiently embryonic to permit some insurers to set a single price for particular categories of people in an entire community, regardless of actual costs generated by different groups. This arrangement, which permitted high-cost groups to be insured at less than their true expected cost, contributed to the reduction in the numbers of uninsured to an all-time low in the late 1970s.

Furthermore, those who were insured at the workplace were often spared outlays at the time of illness and paid little or nothing later because employers paid the full premium.

By the late 1980s, however, the attractiveness of the health care financing system had plummeted for all of these groups, and current trends suggest that the downward slide will continue. Business executives now see health insurance as a major financial threat because the cost is high and growing unpredictably. The slow growth of productivity since the mid-1970s has led to a drop in real take-home pay for the average U.S. worker, and the increasing share of compensation devoted to employer-financed health insurance has contributed to this drop. Furthermore, the Tax Reform Act of 1986, by lowering most people's tax rates, reduced the advantages of personal tax exemption of employer-financed premiums.

In their efforts to control costs, employers have asked insurance companies or other organizations to scrutinize the delivery of health care in ways that restrict the clinical freedom of physicians and frustrate their capacity to do all that they may think medically appropriate. Employers have also tried to control costs by curtailing certain benefits and by boosting the share of premiums paid by employees; these measures increase workers' awareness of costs, but also discourage them from accepting coverage for themselves or their families. The method of paying hospitals used by the federal medicare program no longer permits hospitals to bill for costs incurred, and persistent deficits have led the federal government to restrict the increase in medicare payments. Private insurance companies increasingly bargain with hospitals and physicians for prices tailored to the cost experience of particular employer sponsors. This practice, by reducing the profit providers can earn on most groups, reduces their capacity to care for the uninsured. To an increasing extent, insurance companies have been relegated to the role of bill payers hired by companies to process claims for large groups. And the cost consciousness of all private payers has forced insurance companies to boost premiums or deny coverage altogether to small groups. The intensification of cost consciousness has exposed flaws in private insurance markets that raise doubts about the capacity of this system to serve large segments of the U.S. population under freely competitive conditions.

The Inescapable Debate

A major national debate on restructuring the U.S. system of paying for health care is inescapable during the 1990s. The beginnings of that debate are apparent in the spate of recent proposals to extend health insurance coverage for acute and long-term care and to rein in costs. The reports have only one feature in common: the awareness that the current system is unsustainable and must be changed.

Some proposals support a requirement that employers sponsor health insurance for all or most of their workers or else pay a tax sufficient to provide coverage. Of those who oppose such mandatory employer-sponsored health insurance, some would use measures to remove imperfections in private insurance markets and incentives to encourage employers to sponsor coverage, while others would scrap employer-sponsored insurance and substitute universal government-sponsored insurance. Studies disagree on whether the added costs of extending insurance to those who now lack it should be borne by private companies, by the government, or by varying combinations of the two. Practically everyone supports recent federal government initiatives to evaluate the efficacy of current medical procedures, but some think such studies will significantly slow spending growth, while others regard such hopes as visionary. Some reports urge major reforms in the reimbursement of hospitals and physicians, while others would retain current arrangements. Some reports claim that increases in competition in the health care industry and careful monitoring of care by insurance companies or other experts will significantly slow spending growth, while others claim such initiatives are unlikely to have much effect on costs. The efforts by employers to hold down costs tend to narrow insurance coverage or to reduce providers' capacity to extend care to uninsured patients. As costs continue to rise, the pressures on employers to intensify these efforts will increase.

Controls on spending will tend to reduce insurance coverage, and extending financial access will boost costs. But progress can be made on both goals if they are tackled together. To achieve both goals will require fundamental reforms in the ways in which health insurance is acquired and health care providers are paid. In short, those who are most anxious to curb health care spending must make common cause with those most determined to guarantee everyone some form of health insurance, because neither group will be able to reach its goal without the cooperation of the other.

As is true of all major departures from current federal policy, presidential support is vital. Elections create presidential commitments. The national debate will begin in earnest when an incumbent president or a presidential candidate finds that the erosion of support for the current health care financing system has made reform a politically attractive issue. Meanwhile, various state governments will continue to deal with some of the problems with health care financing, most notably the incompleteness of health insurance coverage.

This book is not a comprehensive review of current health care policy or of health care economics. Rather, it is a selective tour of certain aspects of health care financing and economics that I think are central for an understanding of the debate on reform. Health care is not and cannot be treated in the same fashion as other economic commodities whose allocation is left to relatively unregulated markets. These differences include the overarching fact that many people regard access to basic health care as fundamental to life in modern industrial society. Although the same is true of food, clothing, and shelter, health care differs from other goods for many other reasons I describe in succeeding chapters. Understanding these differences is important for thinking about whether and how the financing of health care should be reformed.

Another theme of this book is that reform will have to build on existing U.S. institutional arrangements—modifying, improving, and extending them, but not scrapping them in favor of some entirely new system. Few people fully appreciate the diversity of the current system and hence of the divergent interests of the various groups it affects. Furthermore, this system is not a caprice of history but the outcome of lengthy evolution and hard-fought battles. For that reason no foreign system can be transplanted intact to the United States. It remains important, however, to understand that other countries have solved the problems of how to finance health care and control costs in a wide variety of ways. Some may prove useful guides to American efforts. Consequently, I compare certain dimensions of the U.S. health care financing system with those found elsewhere.

Finally, I review the broad strategies for reform implicit in the welter of plans that various official and private organizations have recently proposed. I conclude with a proposal designed to achieve each of the major goals for reform. It contains a proposal for a new earmarked tax sufficient to cover federal health care costs, including those now dependent on general revenues. The plan therefore contributes to reduction of the overall federal deficit as well as to control of private health care spending.

My purpose, however, is less to urge one approach to the reform of health care financing than to fuel the debate on how to change the U.S. health care financing system. This purpose is based on my conviction that the persistent failure of the United States to assure everyone access to basic care is inexcusable, and that the failure to think rationally about curbing health care costs is exorbitantly wasteful.

CHAPTER TWO

Economic Issues in Health Care

NO DEVELOPED country relies exclusively on free markets to produce and allocate health care. All rely instead on a mixture of actions by governments and private organizations. This chapter highlights some of the special characteristics of health care services that are relevant to the current debate about financing reform. In particular, numerous vexing problems result because insurance shields most people against most of the costs of acute health care. However, gaps in insurance coverage for a sizable minority of the population also pose serious difficulties. Health care is peculiar in that some of it quite literally makes the difference between life and death, but most consumers are unqualified to evaluate it. Competition in the market for health insurance drives companies to enage in strategies that produce inferior results for the insured population but are necessary for the companies' survival. Each of these issues figures prominently in debates about whether and how to reform the U.S. health care system.[1]

Consumption and Insurance

In most industries, rising sales signal success; in health care, rising expenditures are widely regarded as a problem. The problem arises

1. Another issue, the fear of many U.S. managers that the current U.S. system for financing health care, which is based on employer-sponsored and -financed health

8

because even well-informed patients have little incentive to weigh the benefits and risks of diagnosis or therapy against the full cost of care. In 1989 insurance spared patients more than nine-tenths of the total cost of hospitalization and more than three-fourths of the cost of physicians' services.[2] As a result, patients have every incentive to seek care that they think will bring even modest benefits and have little reason to consider cost.[3] If physicians selflessly executed their patients' wishes, they would render such care. If the added income physicians earn when they prescribe more care were to influence their decisions, they might provide care that produces no benefits at all; and in the absence of clear and widely understood standards for care, they might even provide harmful services.

In short, strong incentives exist for the provision of much health care that in some sense costs more than it is worth.[4] Moreover, as research expands the menu of beneficial diagnostic and therapeutic interventions, the bill for high-cost, low-benefit medicine tends to grow inexorably.

No developed country has escaped this problem. All have decided, through public decisions or private actions, to insulate pa-

---

insurance, puts them at serious disadvantage in international competition, is examined in chapter 4.

2. *HHS News*, December 20, 1990, table 3.

3. I use the term "benefit" to refer to the evaluation by a well-informed patient, aware of the risks and discomfort as well as the possibilities of amelioration or cure, not to the evaluation by some third party, even the physician. Thus a patient who rationally rejects life-saving care because the chances of success are small or discomfort of therapy is too great would, by definition, receive no benefit from therapy. For a moving description of such a case, see Timothy E. Quill, "Death and Dignity: A Case of Individualized Decision Making," *New England Journal of Medicine*, March 7, 1991, pp. 691–94. This definition raises some difficult issues of when patients should be deemed incompetent to decide. It also raises difficulties, explored below, when the patient's own evaluation can be expected to change over the course of a possible therapy. In some cases, society may decide that individuals systematically misperceive benefits and that the least costly way to correct those misperceptions is by making certain services mandatory (vaccinations, for example) or providing them at sharply reduced cost (smoking prevention programs, for example).

4. Exactly how much depends on the pattern of benefits. Insurance does not much affect the splinting of broken bones, the benefits of which are either considerable or negligible. But it substantially increases the number and cost of diagnostic tests, such as computed tomography (CT scans) and blood tests, which provide potentially life-saving information for some patients, important benefits for others, and negligible benefits for many more. See Henry J. Aaron and William B. Schwartz, *The Painful Prescription: Rationing Hospital Care* (Brookings, 1984).

tients, in whole or in part, from the cost of care when ill. In so doing they have encouraged demand for nearly all beneficial care and blunted incentives for efficiency, because patients have little reason to care about needless expense. Without other actions, the result of such systems would be economic waste—the production of health care worth less than other goods and services that could be produced with the same resources. The policy challenge is to counteract the incentives to produce wastefully large quantities of health care at unnecessarily high cost without directly imposing excessive burdens on sick people or their families.

Insurance and Demand for Care

According to standard economic theory, households divide their budgets among commodities, based on well-defined preferences and market prices, so that the last dollar spent on each commodity yields roughly the same satisfaction or "utility." Households thereby derive the maximum possible satisfaction from their incomes. The higher the price of a commodity, the smaller the quantity demanded, as shown by the line DD in figure 2-1. DD may also be regarded as a benefits curve, showing the benefits, ranked from highest to lowest, of each successive dollar spent on health care.[5] Facing the full price of care, patients or physicians acting on their behalf would demand care as long as benefits exceeded cost, shown by the quantity Q_0 in figure 2-1.

Because serious illnesses are infrequent, costly, and unpredictable for individual households, health insurance can improve welfare by enabling people to trade a fixed payment—the insurance premium—for a disturbingly uncertain one—the threat of large medical expenses. The health insurance premium is the sum of the cost of health care and the extra administrative cost of insurance and the insurer's profit, sometimes called the "loading charge." But since people would have to pay the cost of health care in any event, the

5. For a discussion of the application of benefits curves to the efficient allocation of resources to health care, see Aaron and Schwartz, The Painful Prescription. As drawn, figure 2-1 indicates that some people derive very large benefits relative to costs, some receive benefits approximately equal to costs, and many receive small benefits. Health care analysts often refer to care rendered to those who receive meager benefits as "flat of the curve" medicine for obvious geometrical reasons.

Figure 2–1. *The Benefits Curve*

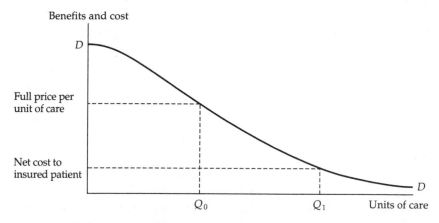

true economic price of insurance—the extra cost incurred to avoid exposure when ill to the full cost of medical care—is simply the loading charge.[6] People will buy insurance if the loading charge is smaller than the value of the gains in security that insurance makes possible.

Health insurance reduces the cost of health care that patients face at the time that care is demanded, but it increases the amount of health care individuals consume and hence the total cost to society at large.[7] If insurance covers, say, 80 percent of the cost of care—what is customarily called 20 percent coinsurance—people typically will demand as much care as they would at a price only one-fifth that of

6. The price of insurance actually includes an additional element. Because insurance reduces the price of care, it thereby leads those who are insured to consume more health care than they would if they were uninsured. Part of health insurance premiums therefore pays for care that is worth less to the insured than the full cost. The difference between the production cost of such care and the value to the insured is also part of the loading charge as far as the insured person is concerned.

7. This consequence of insurance is sometimes called "moral hazard," a term borrowed from property and casualty insurance. Fire insurance, for example, reduces the incentives purchasers of insurance have to install sprinkler systems or to incur other costs to avoid the risk of fire. Insurance thereby increases the risk against which it provides protection, much as health insurance increases total outlays on health care. Moral hazard is a problem in many important markets, including that for labor. Where it is important it invalidates the presumption that competitive markets will lead to economically efficient outcomes. On this issue, see Richard J. Arnott and Joseph E. Stiglitz, "The Basic Analytics of Moral Hazard," and "The Welfare Economics of Moral Hazard," Working Papers 2484, 3316 (Cambridge, Mass.: National Bureau of Economic Research, January 1988, April 1990).

actual charges, the amount shown by Q_1 in figure 2-1.[8] Note that the amount by which use of health care with insurance exceeds use without insurance depends on the shape of the benefits curve DD. If DD is steep, the excess will be small. If DD is relatively flat, the difference could be enormous.[9]

As a result of insurance, the total cost of medical care borne by the patient at the time of illness may rise or fall. But insurance is almost certain to boost the overall cost of health care to all payers, for at least four related reasons to which society may react quite differently. First, insurance boosts demand for care by patients whose long-term incomes are sufficient to pay for care, but who lack sufficient savings to pay for large medical expenses and who are unable or unwilling to borrow to pay for care.[10] Second, insurance boosts demand for types of care, notably preventive services, that produce benefits many patients do not fully appreciate and will demand only if the services are subsidized or free.[11] Third, health insurance encourages people to buy health care, such as vaccinations, that produces benefits not only for the patient but for others and that uninsured patients might not seek because they ignore the benefits to others. Finally, as noted, insurance simply reduces the price of health care and increases the quantity demanded even when the benefits all accrue entirely to the patient or the patient's family and there is no social interest in the benefits.

Various people are likely to disagree about the social importance of increases in demand for health care from each source. In particular, a good case can be made that increases in demand are

8. "Coinsurance" refers to the percentage of each dollar of cost the patient must pay. Alternatively, patients may be required to bear some of the cost of health care by "deductibles," which are fixed charges they must pay before insurance applies, or through "copayments," fixed charges per unit of service.

9. Some people carry more than one insurance policy and can actually recover more than the full cost of treatment. In such cases, the net cost to an insured patient would fall below the x-axis, indicating that all beneficial therapy and even, possibly, some harmful therapy would be sought. Alternatively, such overinsured patients may regard the excess reimbursement as analogous to judgments awarded to tort victims for pain and suffering and consciously seek to be overinsured for this reason.

10. In economic terms, insurance can remove "liquidity constraints."

11. Preventive care holds out the potential to cut total health care spending if the care that is avoided through the prevention of illness exceeds the cost of the preventive measures. This potential is seldom realized in practice because many people must be educated or tested for each case of the illness prevented. On this issue, see Louise B. Russell, *Is Prevention Better Than Cure?* (Brookings, 1986).

socially desirable for services that are undervalued, that have important effects on other people, or that a lack of ready cash prevents patients from seeking, while increases in demand because insurance cuts out-of-pocket costs to patients below production cost probably are often not desirable. The curve DD in figure 2-1 does not distinguish among the various types of added demand that insurance induces. A major task of health care policy is to fashion incentives that preserve meritorious increases in demand but curtail the low- or no-benefit increases.

Most countries have resolved this dilemma by providing health insurance to essentially all residents or citizens and by controlling costs through budget limits that force hospitals and physicians to set priorities on what equipment to buy and which services to provide (see chapter 4). They also set fee schedules or other restrictions on expenditures on physicians' services.

An implicit and somewhat controversial implication of figure 2-1 is that the benefits of some health care are worth less than they cost to produce. By inference, such health care is not worth having and society would benefit from its elimination. This implication runs counter to the view, heard more often in the past than currently, that human life has infinite value and any expenditure that improves health or extends life of acceptable quality is desirable.

Decisions made every day contradict this pious sentiment. Roads and automobiles are not engineered to achieve maximum safety. Society allows such environmental hazards as polluted air and water to persist. Adults may elect to forgo tamper-proof caps and thereby increase the risk that children will accidentally consume medicines. The laundry room and garage of virtually every house contain potentially lethal tools and chemicals. In these and countless other cases, people consciously accept risks because avoiding them is just too costly or inconvenient.

Physicians: The Patient's Agent?

All business owners, including sellers of professional services, are assumed to be in business to make a profit. They are subject to laws barring fraud and governing contracts. Most businesses place a considerable value on a reputation for honesty and consideration of the customers' interests, but violators are punished by the courts or by the market, if at all. Lawyers, accountants, and medical care providers are also subject to codes of professional ethics that call upon them to act in the best interest of their clients.[12] Clients are assumed to be unable, because of ignorance, illness, or some other condition, to fully evaluate the professional's performance and to discipline derelictions of responsibility. Accordingly, egregious violations of ethics can cause professional organizations to disqualify a member from staying in business.

Considerable doubt has arisen as to whether all physicians adhere to this standard consistently. Many investigators have observed that physicians have, and use, the power to induce demand for their own services.[13] Medical outlays are relatively high where physicians are relatively numerous. But this pattern could easily arise because of local conditions that cause strong demand for medical care and attract many physicians. One cannot be confident that physicians have or use the power to create demand for their own services without careful statistical analysis. Solid statistical confirmation of physician-induced demand is unlikely.[14] The problem is that proof requires successful statistical controls of all factors, other than the number of physicians, that might influence the demand of care. Data adequate to meet this test are unlikely to ever be available. Victor R. Fuchs has argued that evidence of physician-induced demand is adequate for reasonable observers.[15]

12. Kenneth J. Arrow, "Uncertainty and the Welfare Economics of Medical Care," *American Economic Review*, vol. 53 (December 1963), pp. 941–73. See also Arnott and Stiglitz, "The Basic Analytics of Moral Hazard," and "The Welfare Economics of Moral Hazard."

13. For an agnostic evaluation of the literature on physician-induced demand, see Charles E. Phelps, "Induced Demand—Can We Ever Know Its Extent?" *Journal of Health Economics*, vol. 5 (December 1986), pp. 355–65.

14. To illustrate the problem, a study carried out by Abt Associates found that physicians who do their own radiologic studies prescribe such tests 4 to 4.5 times more often and charge higher fees than do physicians who refer their patients to radiologists. The authors adjusted for case mix. This result establishes that physicians who own their own radiologic equipment do more tests than do physicians who do not own such equipment. But it does not establish whether they are using too many diagnostic tests or physicians who do not own such equipment are using too few. See Bruce J. Hillman and others, "Frequency and Costs of Diagnostic Imaging in Office Practice—A Comparison of Self-Referring and Radiologist-Referring Physicians," *New England Journal of Medicine*, December 6, 1990, pp. 1604–08.

15. By analogy, Fuchs cites the story of "the Frenchman who suspected that his wife was unfaithful. When [the Frenchman] told his friend that the uncertainty was ruining his life, the friend suggested hiring a private detective to resolve the matter

Whatever power physicians have to determine demand for their own services stems from at least two facts. First, a small minority of very sick patients account for most health care expenditures (see chapter 3). Seriously ill patients often cannot review the appropriateness of care. Second, and more generally, patients frequently do not know what diagnostic procedures or therapeutic measures are necessary: that is one reason they go to doctors. Physicians use the power over demand, it is alleged, to increase their incomes. Repeat visits, extra tests, extra therapy, or even surgery all generate additional income for the physician, but the patient is often unable to judge their necessity.[16]

If all medical procedures were subject to hard scientific validation, if physicians always provided full information to patients, and if patients were able and willing to use such information and participate actively in decisions about their own care, the failure of physicians to act as faithful agents for their patients would be easy to detect and therefore rare. None of these conditions is satisfied, however. Scientific criteria are often lacking for when diagnoses should be performed, how many tests are enough, and which therapies should be employed. This lack is one of the reasons advanced to explain enormous variations in the rate at which common medical procedures are performed in geographic areas that are seemingly similar

---

once and for all. He did so, and a few days later the detective came and gave his report: 'One evening when you were out of town I saw your wife get dressed in a slinky black dress, put on perfume, and go down to the local bar. She had several drinks with the piano player and when the bar was closed they came back to your house. They sat in the living room, had a few more drinks, danced, and kissed.' The Frenchman listened intently as the detective went on: 'Then they went upstairs to the bedroom, they playfully undressed one another, and got into bed. Then they put out the light and I could see no more.' The Frenchman sighed, 'Always that doubt, always that doubt.' " "Physician-Induced Demand: A Parable," *Journal of Health Economics*, vol. 5 (December 1986), p. 367.

16. Commenting on the view that patients can effectively monitor the behavior of physicians, Uwe E. Reinhardt remarks: "In any given year, the bulk of all health expenditures are made in the names of a relative few, probably fairly sick, individuals. The belief that overall health care expenditures can be effectively controlled by these sick human beings at the nexus between patients and providers seems to be uniquely American and, even within the United States, uniquely incident upon the economics profession, whence the idea originated. . . .[This view] suggests a remarkable faith in the ability of frail, [often] elderly persons struck by illness to function as vigilant, rational health care shoppers, capable of disciplining wayward doctors and hospitals." Comments on Bengt Jönsson, "What Can Americans Learn from Europeans?" *Health Care Financing Review, 1989 Annual Supplement*, p. 101.

and near one another.[17] Physicians vary widely in the amount of information they think patients should receive. And patients vary widely in their capacity to absorb such information, in their tastes for treatment, and in their willingness or even desire to let others make decisions for them. In practice, the care many patients want depends on the information their physician provides and on how it is tendered. For that reason, even if physicians invariably tried to do everything that their patients would wish, but no more, the design of incentives for both patients and providers would still be a complex problem. Insurance encourages physicians who are acting in their patients' interests to provide relatively low-benefit care, as indicated in figure 2-1. What steps, if any, should be taken to mute those incentives in order to control the cost of health care?

Changing Circumstances and Changing Tastes

Standard economic analysis holds that consumer choice in free markets enables people to maximize the welfare that a given amount of income can provide them. Central to this line of argument is the assumption that people have well-defined and stable preferences.

The argument that consumer decisions maximize consumer welfare as they see it is almost tautological for goods that are consumed immediately—if some allocation of expenditures were superior to the one chosen, the consumer would have chosen the alternative.[18] Furthermore, the gain in welfare from free consumer choice is thought to be large. In the short run, consumers are best able to

17. The pioneer in studying variations in use of medical care among small areas is John E. Wennberg. See, for example, John E. Wennberg and Alan Gittelsohn, "Small Area Variation in Health Care Delivery," *Science*, December 14, 1973, pp. 1102–08. Use of procedures under medicare varies enormously. See John Holahan, Robert A. Berenson, and Peter G. Kachavos, "Area Variations in Selected Medicare Procedures," *Health Affairs*, vol. 9 (Winter 1990), pp. 166–75. For a summary of studies of small-area variations in care and of the possible causes of these variations, see Charles E. Phelps and Cathleen Mooney, "Variations in Medical Practice Use: Causes and Consequences," University of Rochester, June 8, 1990.

18. Not all commodities fit this mold, of course. By common agreement, people are not allowed to choose less than stipulated quantities of elementary and secondary education for their children or of public health services for themselves and their families. In the case of most goods, however, consumers are seen as better positioned than anyone else to decide what to buy.

match available goods against their own preferences. In the longer run, consumer choices guide producers to design and introduce goods and services that fulfill consumers' desires increasingly well. Consumers are more likely to make mistakes in purchasing goods that last a long time, particularly if circumstances change between purchase and consumption. In particular, tastes may change after the purchase of such durable goods as houses or automobiles. Usually consumers can correct such "mistakes" by trading up or down.

Health insurance and health care pose special problems, however. Health insurance typically is purchased by healthy people, while most health care is consumed by sick people. In contrast to people purchasing durable consumer goods, sick people cannot normally replace health insurance that once seemed optimal but no longer does.[19] Should the selection of a particular health insurance plan be regarded as optimal because it reflected the consumer's free choice when the original decision was made? Or, in situations where tastes of the sick consumer of health care have changed, should the earlier decision be regarded as inferior?

These issues are more than academic, and they are likely to grow in immediacy as concerns about rising health care costs intensify. Under the pressure of rising costs, employer-sponsors will be tempted to offer workers plans that cover different sets of benefits, thereby allowing workers to choose a plan that seems most useful at the time the choice is made. Current legal doctrine regarding living wills and durable powers of attorney illustrates the importance of changes in tastes.[20] Law stipulates that a person may revoke such documents at any time and in any way and may not be questioned legally on such a decision.[21]

19. Plans that offer a choice in coverage typically permit employees to change plans no more than once a year during a so-called open season. This limitation serves precisely to prevent sick people from switching from one plan to another that has better coverage for their current illness.

20. Living wills allow individuals to stipulate what medical interventions they desire in specified medical circumstances. Typically, living wills are used to avoid aggressive therapy in circumstances where the maker of the will would wish limited care or none at all. Durable powers of attorney permit a person to appoint another person to make binding decisions about medical care if the signer of the power of attorney is incapable of doing so.

21. This practice embodies an acute sensitivity to the possibility that preferences expressed by a healthy person about medical care in the event of illness should not

People are not allowed to change their minds at will about insurance, however. A young one-earner couple on a tight budget may decide to forgo optional health insurance coverage for dependents and use the additional take-home pay for added consumption or to support an aged parent. After the premature birth of a child with multiple illnesses and developmental disabilities, the same couple may feel rather differently. A healthy couple in their sixties may see little point in paying the premium for long-term-care insurance, but change their minds after learning that one spouse suffers from Alzheimer's disease, at which point most insurance companies would refuse to offer coverage. In each case, the people may have correctly understood the probabilities of the events in question and decided coolly and rationally to take a gamble they later regret. The point of these examples is not that the decision was erroneous when made, nor does it hinge on the decision to forgo coverage: the examples could have been based on a decision, later regretted, to buy extensive coverage.

Rather, the examples indicate that, contrary to the usual postulates of welfare economics, values may be conditioned on circumstances.[22] Society normally has little interest when people gamble and lose. But when the gamble concerns events that change basic preferences and that affect the life and health of oneself and one's family, it is not clear why past consumer decisions deserve priority over new preferences.[23]

---

bind that same person in any way if the reality of illness or anything else causes a change of heart. Yet medical ethicist Daniel Callahan holds that people should collectively make binding commitments when young and healthy to forgo costly life-extending health care for themselves when elderly, provided that improved long-term care and palliative acute care become available. See "Correspondence: Rationing Medical Care," *New England Journal of Medicine,* January 17, 1991, pp. 194–95. Decisions to deny the wishes of people who might want care would be more defensible if based on evaluations of net medical benefit and applied equally to members of every age group. Even if one accepts such an approach, however, it does not justify any separate consideration of the age of the patient, unless one holds that the very act of living to a certain age reduces one's claim on health care resources.

22. The circumstances under which values evolve systematically with events are common. For an explanation of how this circumstance can lead to seriously inferior results, see George Akerlof, "Procrastination and Obedience," *American Economic Review,* vol. 81 (May 1991, *Papers and Proceedings, 1990*), pp. 1–19.

23. Thomas Schelling put the point sharply. "A few years ago, I saw again, after nearly fifty years, the original *Moby Dick.* . . . Ahab, in a bunk below deck after his

The implication of such possible shifts in consumer preferences is not that variability in the character of health plans is always useless or perverse and that consumers would be better off without choice. The contrary is true. Many differences among health plans resemble the normal variation in other consumer goods. But changes in circumstances reduce both the advantages of private choice and the inefficiencies that usually result when public decisions block consumer choice. They strengthen the case for public determination of the main elements that every health insurance plan must contain (and, perhaps, of certain components that no plan may contain). Such collective decisions do not demonstrably violate consumer choice as would, say, requirements about what people could eat, wear, or read. In fact, private group health insurance typically circumscribes options available to employees, even when a menu of options is available. The opportunity for individuals to choose among certain optional insurance coverages could be preserved as well within a national or state plan as it is within employer-sponsored plans. The harder question concerns how much choice it is desirable to retain in both.

The Fuzzy Benefits Curve

Although the benefits curve, DD, in figure 2-1 is drawn as a well-defined line, it is actually poorly defined. First, medical benefits take many forms, including physical cure, reduction of pain, and

---

leg has been severed by the whale, watches the ship's blacksmith approach with a red-hot iron which, only slightly cooled by momentary immersion in a bucket of water, is to cauterize his stump. As three seamen hold him, he pleads not to be burnt, begging in horror as the blacksmith throws back the blanket. And as the iron touches his body he spews out the apple that he has been chewing, in the most awful scream that at age twelve I had ever heard. Nobody doubts that the sailors who held him did what they had to do, and the blacksmith too. When the story resumes there is no sign he regrets having been cauterized or bears any grievance toward the men who, rather than defend him against the hot iron, held him at the blacksmith's mercy. . . . If I say that in Ahab's condition I would like to be cauterized, you will notice that I say it with a fearlessness that makes my decision suspect. . . . After you burn me and I recover and thank you, you give me the bad news: the other leg is infected and must be burned the same way. . . . Do I withdraw my thanks, for fear you'll think I want it done again? . . . The question entails the kind of undecidability that many economists attribute to the interpersonal comparison of utilities." *Choice and Consequence: Perspectives of an Errant Economist* (Harvard University Press, 1984), pp. 83, 92.

psychological comfort. Because various health care providers and patients value each of these benefits differently, no unambiguous index of overall medical benefit exists. Second, knowledge about the actual effects of various medical interventions is grossly deficient. Even the quantity of medical services is not well defined. When length of stay in a hospital is reduced because improved postoperative procedures permit more rapid healing, has the quantity of care rendered to a patient risen or fallen, and how should the change be measured?[24]

Indeed, economists usually focus on demand for, rather than benefits of, ordinary commodities. They assume, sometimes rather arbitrarily, that the benefits from the last unit of goods consumers buy are roughly proportional to cost. In the case of medical care, no such assumption is justified, for two related reasons: physicians, not consumers, largely determine patient care, and the rate at which various diagnostic and therapeutic procedures are used varies widely. If physicians in each area provided services first to those who stand to benefit most from care and used different cutoff points in deciding which patients would derive benefits too small to justify intervention, care would be inefficiently distributed among patients, but the benefits curve would be well defined. But large variations in care persist largely because most commonly used medical procedures have never been tested in a clinical setting, medical schools differ somewhat in the style of practice they teach their students, and practice customs vary from place to place.[25]

The implication of the fuzzy benefits curve and the large variations

24. If the quantity of health care is poorly defined, so is the price, since expenditures, which are clearly defined, exactly equal price per unit of care times quantity of care. On this issue, see chapter 3. This problem of definition is not unique to medical services. What is the unit of service from one hour of legal consultation? Even videocassette recorders produce benefits of various kinds that various users weight differently. This circumstance has led some economists to treat economic goods as bundles of attributes, rather than as one-dimensional entities. See Kelvin Lancaster, *Consumer Demand: A New Approach* (Columbia University Press, 1971).

25. Phelps and Mooney examine whether differences in care could be attributable to variations in demand by patients or in supply of hospital beds and physicians, to intrinsic differences in patterns of illness, to substitution of some medical procedures for others, or to random events. They conclude that all of these factors taken together cannot explain more than a small part of observed variation in frequency of such procedures as hysterectomy, coronary artery bypass grafts, admissions to hospitals for low back pain, and insertion of pacemakers. See Phelps and Mooney, "Variations in Medical Practice Use."

in care is that medical resources are almost certainly used inefficiently. That is, if good information were available on efficacy and if
this information led to a narrowing of the apparently wide variation
in practice styles, medical benefits per dollar spent could be significantly increased. The fact that the benefits curve is fuzzy does *not*
mean that expenditures on medical care are too high or too low. To
reach such a judgment would require improved information about
the benefits of the most common and most costly interventions, and
society would have to reach some consensus on which benefits are
too small to be worth the cost of providing them. Neither of these
conditions is close to being satisfied.

Implications: Waste or Rationing?

The pervasiveness of insurance creates powerful incentives for
individuals to consume health care for which the social cost exceeds
the social benefit, as illustrated in figure 2-1. Because of the diversity
of illnesses, health care services produce a continuum of benefits
ranging from the complete cure of life-threatening illnesses, followed
by the sustenance of high-quality life, to meager relief or brief extensions of pain-ridden life. This continuum is represented by the line
DD in figure 2-1. Reimbursing on a fee-for-service basis encourages
providers not only to meet all patient demands for care that provides
benefits as large as costs but also to render low-benefit care and
perhaps care promising no net benefits at all. This problem would
be controllable if people could be bound by insurance contracts or
other arrangements established before the onset of illness. Such
contracts would hinge on hard and stable information about what
interventions provide what benefits in what circumstances. Such
information, in general, is not available. But even if it were, it is not
clear that such controls would be desirable if people's tastes when
sick differ in major ways from their tastes when well.

In this difficult situation, private businesses, insurance companies, and governments try to control costs in various ways. They
require reviews of appropriateness of care, promote health maintenance organizations, encourage competition among providers and
insurance vendors, and embrace managed care.[26] Each of these ar-

26. Health maintenance organizations (HMOs) are groups of physicians who contract to provide patients with a broad range of medical services, including hospitaliza-

rangements attempts to limit the effect of the incentive on patients to overconsume and on physicians to oversupply care.

Nevertheless, the total cost of personal health care services has risen as fast since the advent of these efforts to control costs as it did before. Many forces affect the cost of health care: the size and the age of the population, the progress of medical technology, and the price of resources used. Consequently, one cannot validly infer the ineffectiveness of cost control efforts from the continued rise in health costs. Without the various cost control efforts, the increase in costs might have accelerated. At a minimum, however, the sustained rise in costs raises doubt about the efficacy of these cost control efforts and places the burden of proof on those who believe these controls have had much effect. Furthermore, the rapid proliferation of new technologies ensures continued growth of the menu of services providing a continuum of benefits from large to meager.[27]

The various measures already implemented to control costs aim to do so in two ways: by promoting efficiency in the provision of beneficial care and by rationing—that is, by curtailing the provision of care for which benefits are smaller in some sense than total costs. If the cost of health care continues to rise at a rate Americans regard as excessive, then the United States, like all other nations where most residents are insured, will have to decide whether to implement additional arrangements to ration care.

In short, health insurance creates incentives that directly explain

---

tion, for a given period of time for a fixed premium (and minimal cost sharing), regardless of use of medical services. The physicians may be paid on a fee-for-service basis and operate from dispersed offices with patients free to choose among the member physicians ("independent practice associations"). Alternatively, the HMO may hire a closed panel of physicians who are paid on salary (the "staff model"). Under managed care, some individual or group must review care prospectively or retrospectively to make sure that care is necessary and no more costly than is medically necessary. These reviews may include requirements of second opinions before surgery is approved, prior authorization for admission to a hospital or treatment by a specialist, the use of primary-care physicians as "gatekeepers" to screen patients before referral to specialists, and the maintenance of profiles on the use of tests, hospitalization, and drugs by physicians. For a detailed review of managed care, see Congressional Budget Office, *Managed Care and the Medicare Program: Background and Evidence*, CBO Staff Memorandum (May 1990).

27. Henry J. Aaron and William B. Schwartz, "Rationing Health Care: The Choice before Us," *Science*, January 26, 1990, pp. 418–22; and Natalie Angier, "Crucial Gene Is Discovered in Detecting Colon Cancer," *New York Times*, March 15, 1991, p. A1.

the growth of questionable outlays on medical care. The central challenge of reform of health care financing is to preserve financial access for those who now have it and extend it to those who now lack it, but simultaneously to slow the growth of expenditures on low-benefit care. In meeting this challenge, planners should realize that the normal presumption about the optimality of decisions reached through free markets does not fully carry over to decisions about the amounts and kinds of health insurance and health care. Furthermore, they should realize that since insurance by its very nature encourages demand for covered services, efforts to control costs will have to rest on direct restrictions on supply.

Production

The term "personal health care services" encompasses a bewildering variety of activities designed to help people achieve the health status that they want.[28] The delivery of these services is mediated directly through markets for services of hospitals, physicians, and other health professionals and indirectly through labor markets for all of the occupations employed in the delivery of care and product markets for medical devices, equipment, pharmaceuticals, and supplies. Reform of the financing of health care services must take account of the need to preserve incentives for efficient production and innovation in each of these markets.

Incentives for Efficiency and Innovation

Profit maximization creates strong incentives for producers of most commodities to offer goods of given quality at the lowest possible price. To achieve this goal, producers must innovate and minimize costs of production. Technological change results partly from

28. Personal health care services do not include a multiplicity of other individual and collective actions, such as public health measures to ensure clean water, food, and air, to vaccinate children, or to require people to wear seat belts, which together affect health status more than do conventional medical services. The leading cause of death among blacks aged 15 to 24 is murder. Seth Mydans, "Homicide Rate Up for Young Blacks," *New York Times*, December 7, 1990, p. A1. Successful efforts to reduce violence among young black males would do more to extend their life expectancy than would any conceivable medical intervention.

experience acquired in producing a particular kind of output, partly in response to market incentives, and partly from random and unpredictable scientific discoveries. If labor productivity in a particular industry rises faster than the economywide average, the price of that industry's output will tend to fall relative to the general price level; if productivity rises less than average, the relative price will tend to rise.[29]

The production of health care is subject to a number of special problems, quite apart from the fact that the major health care providers, physicians, play an important part in deciding how much of their services and those of other providers patients will use. A pivotal issue concerns the relationship between the rate of technical advance and the method of paying for health care.

Technological Change

An abundance of research indicates that the social returns to most expenditures on research and development are far higher than returns on other investments.[30] The explanation most commonly advanced for this inequality is that expenditures on research and development frequently generate benefits to companies or people other than those who initiate them.[31] Those who pay for research presumably decide how much to spend on the basis of returns they receive, not benefits to others; and if they are averse to risk, they may even discount expected benefits from something as risky as basic research.

The excess of social over private returns to research justifies patent

29. If productivity is constant, the relative price of the commodity tends to rise at a rate equal to the growth of labor productivity in the overall economy, multiplied by labor's share of total revenue. William J. Baumol and William G. Bowen, *Performing Arts: The Economic Dilemma* (New York: Twentieth Century Fund, 1966).

30. Zvi Griliches, "Returns to Research and Development Expenditures in the Private Sector," in John W. Kendrick and Beatrice N. Vaccara, eds., *New Developments in Productivity Measurement and Analysis* (University of Chicago Press, 1980), pp. 419–54. Ariel Pakes and Mark Schankerman found lower returns than Griliches because of the lag between investment in research and commercial payoff and because of rapid obsolescence of the findings of research. See "The Rate of Obsolescence of Patents, Research Gestation Lags, and the Private Rate of Return to Research Resources," in Zvi Griliches, ed., *R&D, Patents, and Productivity* (University of Chicago Press, 1984), pp. 73–88.

31. In economic terms, new knowledge is a "public good."

awards and government support of research. Patents reward successful research by allowing inventors a monopoly of limited duration and the chance to make sufficient profits to reward the uncertainties of research. The drawback of patents is that they restrict the application of knowledge that could be put to wider use. Government grants reduce private costs and thereby encourage research that would not otherwise take place. Both patents and grants are used to encourage medical research.

Patents are not available, in general, for clinical innovations, and until recently few grants were awarded to test established medical procedures. Ethical concerns also hinder evaluation of commonly used procedures because standard research procedures entail comparing two groups of patients, one that receives the treatment and one that does not. This method of evaluation, which is also used to evaluate new drugs, minimizes the chances that approved procedures or drugs will be dangerous or ineffectual. But it is costly and it also delays the introduction of procedures that are eventually found to be safe and effective, thereby depriving patients of beneficial interventions during the testing period. Thus a trade-off exists between safety and delay in availability. Because of variations in both the risks from new therapies and the potential benefits from their introduction, optimal testing procedures are also certain to differ from case to case. For example, protests by AIDS activists have led the Food and Drug Administration to shorten testing procedures for certain new methods of treating AIDS.[32] Few people and no government agencies are willing to deny patients commonly used treatments that are thought to be effective, even if the scientific basis for belief in efficacy is flimsy.

The financing of medical care also influences private investments in research on new drugs, equipment, and therapies. If patients are heavily insured and bear little or no cost for added care, new procedures will be prescribed whenever the incremental benefit exceeds the cost the patient faces. A private company trying to decide

32. Current procedures took approximately their existing form in response to deformities caused by the drug thalidomide. Sam Peltzman has presented evidence that the price for increased safety and efficacy, paid in the form of of reduced research because of increased testing costs and delayed introduction of new drugs, may be excessive. See Sam Peltzman, "An Evaluation of Consumer Protection Legislation: The 1962 Drug Amendments," *Journal of Political Economy*, vol. 81 (September–October 1973), pp. 1049–91.

whether to initiate research is assured that it will have a market for any product that is even modestly beneficial. If spending for health care were restricted, in contrast, sales prospects for new products would also be limited. For this reason, effective controls on medical care spending promise not only to reduce outlays directly, but also to hold down growth of medical spending over time by slowing medical research.[33]

Such analyses have led economists to two conclusions. The first is that, left to their own devices, free markets produce too little research to maximize social welfare. The second is that the tendency for too little to be spent on research can be offset by measures that transfer to society part of the costs of research: patents, which enable investigators to make others pay them for the social benefits of their successful research, or tax incentives or other subsidies, which shift part of the cost of privately managed research to public budgets. Health insurance encourages medical research in an additional way, by increasing the size of the market for beneficial innovations (see figure 2-1).

Innovation in medical care has accelerated since 1953, when Francis Crick and James D. Watson identified the components and geometry of genes, and is still growing. Genetic research has advanced understanding of the functioning of cells and their components and promises breakthroughs in treatments of major physical and mental diseases. Medical technologies that did not exist two or three decades ago account for the bulk of medical expenditures and explain most of the rise in health care spending (see chapter 3).

Some observers have called for reductions in the amount or changes in the character of biomedical research support as a method of slowing growth of spending on health care. This recommendation is shortsighted and flawed; indeed, increased support for biomedical research would probably be in the nation's interest. To the extent that biomedical research results in new devices and techniques that produce substantial benefits, society gains from their introduction. The problem is that current methods of reimbursement underwrite

---

33. Joseph P. Newhouse, "The Structure of Health Insurance and the Erosion of Competition in the Medical Marketplace," in Warren Greenberg, ed., *Competition in the Health Care Sector: Past, Present, and Future* (Germantown, Md.: Aspen Systems Corp., 1978), pp. 270–87; and Newhouse, "Has the Erosion of the Medical Marketplace Ended?" *Journal of Health Politics, Policy, and Law,* vol. 13 (Summer 1988), pp. 263–77.

not only the highly beneficial uses of new technology but also those that are marginally beneficial. Scientific advance steadily intensifies the need to reform health care financing in order to curtail low-benefit care and to improve knowledge about when various therapies yield large benefits.

Competition and the Market for Health Insurance

Nobody is neutral about the role of competition in the provision and financing of health care. Some see it as the salvation from rising costs and a guarantor of quality. Others see it as an unachievable fantasy.

The "health care industry" is a large collection of markets producing highly diverse economic goods and services. People and businesses buy health insurance from nearly 650 insurance companies (including 78 Blue Cross and Blue Shield plans). They use this insurance, their own money, and benefits under numerous federal and state programs to buy services from physicians, hospitals, health maintenance organizations, clinics, and a bewildering panoply of other health care providers. Patients and providers use the services of nurses, physician assistants, and other health care support personnel, and the products of pharmaceutical companies, device and equipment manufacturers, and other suppliers.

Some markets involved in the financing and delivery of personal health care services resemble the idealized perfectly competitive market populated by many buyers and sellers, all of whom are well informed and take a market price as given. Many companies manufacture medical equipment and build hospital structures; many hospitals and physicians compete to hire nurses and hospital technicians in a labor market much like that for computer programmers or carpenters. In contrast, the market for pharmaceutical products is characterized by patent-based monopolies. The market for insurance is subject to governmental regulation designed to ensure financial soundness of vendors. Still other markets, notably those for the direct provision of patient care by physicians and hospitals, combine intense competition (as when hospitals or groups of physicians bid against one another to be preferred providers for large insured groups) and market power verging on that of monopoly (as when a particular patient who is fully insured relies on a particular physician for advice about what services are appropriate).

Given this diversity, discussions of the potential role of competition would be far more fruitful if they focused on particular health care markets. To what extent can competition improve the operation of particular markets? In which markets is it likely to be impracticable or harmful? In the market for hospital services, for example, competition can take the form of efforts to operate at least cost and set charges as low as possible to cover costs. Or it can take the form of efforts by each hospital to provide a full range of services even when the market in the community could be served adequately if hospitals specialized and reduced redundant and costly capacity.

In the market for health insurance, competition brings important benefits and formidable costs. The critical question in reforming the financing of health care is whether to try to promote competition in a private health insurance market by changing elements that restrict coverage and hinder cost control, or to scrap competition and rely on other means of providing insurance coverage.

Benefits of Competitive Insurance Markets

Diversity of insurance plans and providers brings significant benefits. First, Americans can match insurance to preferences by selecting among plans of equivalent cost but with different features. This advantage is realized fully only for workers whose employers offer a wide range of plans and who have the information and skills to select wisely.

Second, competition among insurers may improve service and foster innovation. For example, insurance companies have encouraged groups of physicians to form independent practice associations (IPAs) that provide a stipulated range of services to patients for a fee fixed at the start of each year.[34] They have promoted measures to

34. Patients typically pay a fixed fee for stipulated services through an IPA, just as under HMOs. Physicians who agree to provide services through an IPA normally continue to practice separately and to bill the IPA on a fee-for-service basis, in contrast to staff HMOs, in which physicians practice at an HMO-owned facility and are paid on a salary basis. Any excess of IPA premiums is shared in some fashion among providers at the end of the year. Deficits are handled by the creation of reserves or

reduce costs, including managed care. They have cooperated in orga-
nizing hospitals or physicians into preferred provider organizations
(PPOs).[35] Indeed, these innovations form the basis for claims that
competition in a private insurance market will succeed in stopping
growth of low-benefit, high-cost care.

The record to date gives little reason for optimism that competition
will succeed in this objective. The use of PPOs, membership in HMOs
and IPAs, efforts by business purchasers of health insurance to hold
down premiums, and managed care all expanded greatly during the
1980s. Significant reductions in the rate of hospitalization occurred,
although it is unclear whether this trend reflected changes in medical
technology or efforts to control costs. Through all of this, the growth
of total health care spending showed no sign of decelerating (see
chapter 3). To be sure, total health care spending is a crude indicator
of success or failure in controlling growth of low-benefit care. All of
the increase in expenditures may be for services that are worth what
they cost. However, recent studies of efficacy document continued
excessive use of selected medical interventions.[36]

Although the various market-based efforts to hold down growth
of low-benefit, high-cost health spending may be more successful in
the future than they have been in the past, as their supporters
claim, the structural characteristics of insurance make such success
improbable. They contain no device for limiting the flow of resources
to medical care except by curtailing demand. Most medical services
require resources—surgical time, pharmaceutical products, and
nursing care, for example—that will be physically available at the

---

reductions in payments to providers. Evidence indicates that IPAs are as costly as
regular fee-for-service providers.

35. PPOs are groups of physicians, clinics, hospitals, or other health care providers
who contract to provide a defined menu of services to a specified population at lower
than customary rates. Frequently, service from a PPO is an option under employer-
sponsored insurance; if employees agree to take service from members of the PPO,
they are spared some of the cost sharing required of those who use services from
other providers.

36. Based on a number of studies, Robert H. Brook and Mary E. Vaiana report the
overprovision of coronary angiography, carotid endarterectomy, endoscopy of the
upper gastrointestinal tract, coronary artery bypass surgery, pacemaker implantation,
and inappropriate hospitalization. *Appropriateness of Care: A Chart Book*, report prepared
for George Washington University, National Health Policy Forum (Washington, June
1989), p. 4.

time of each individual illness. Since insured patients and physicians acting in their interests will always have strong incentives to make use of these resources, all methods of controlling expenditures will have to rely on private regulatory mechanisms, such as those used under managed care, to blunt the incentives of patients and physicians. Public regulations have failed when they have tried to prevent private decisionmakers from acting in their own interests. Regulations to limit expenditures on costly medical equipment are a prime example. There is no reason to think that private regulations will be any more successful when they try to frustrate the demands of sick patients, who bear little of the cost of their own treatment, and of physicians acting for those patients.

Costs of Competition

Multiple insurers generate administrative costs in their competition to maintain or expand their share of the market. Employers who offer more than one health plan pay to provide information and to help employees choose among these plans. Hospitals and physicians must cope with many payers who follow different rules and require different information. And employees must bear still other costs to master the various systems. Each of these costs would be reduced significantly if insurance were uniform and providers dealt with one payer. They would be reduced still further if hospitals operated on fixed budgets that did not require separate billing for individual patients. Although separate billing does produce an important benefit—information to monitor the quality of care—the cost is high. Total out-of-pocket administrative costs in 1990 may run $50 billion or more.[37]

In addition, competition causes companies to exclude certain pre-

37. One study placed the extra costs of the U.S. system relative to one with a single payer at $29.2 billion in 1983, or 12 percent of the combined outlay on hospitals, physicians, and nursing homes. The corresponding cost for 1990 would be just over $50 billion if the relative costs of administration were unchanged since 1983. See David U. Himmelstein and Steffie Woolhandler, "Cost without Benefit: Administrative Waste in U.S. Health Care," *New England Journal of Medicine*, February 13, 1986, pp. 441–45. These estimates do not include nonmonetary costs, such as time spent by individuals in filing claims or in choosing among insurance options. Nor does it include the costs incurred by businesses in negotiating insurance plans, counseling employees, and handling other insurance issues.

existing conditions from coverage or to impose waiting periods before new employees are covered. These practices cause some people to be uninsured. Such exclusions also hinder job mobility when workers or covered family members have illnesses subject to such conditions. Some private plans provide few or no benefits for certain risks, thereby leaving ostensibly insured patients effectively without insurance for part of their medical outlays. The potential importance of this problem is growing with the emergence of techniques to screen people for predispositions to a wide range of diseases.

Finally, the existence of large numbers of payers, each of whom is typically responsible for only a part of the revenue of any provider, means that no payer has as much leverage over providers as would a single buyer. Although cooperative action to curtail growth of costs is possible, it is costly to organize and seldom happens. Furthermore, coordinated efforts by private payers to control costs may violate antitrust laws.

Experience Rating

Expected medical costs differ widely among individuals categorized by clearly identifiable personal characteristics. For example, medical costs tend to be higher for the elderly than for prime-age adults, for women of childbearing age than for men of the same age, for persons with a history of illness than for the persistently healthy, and for residents of certain regions and communities and workers in certain industries or occupations.

Insurance companies operating in free competitive markets cannot ignore these cost differences. For many years Blue Cross and Blue Shield companies tried to do so. They typically offered insurance within particular geographical areas at a few "community rates" based on the average cost of care for broad classes of customers, such as individuals and families. As commercial companies entered the market for health insurance, they typically set different premiums based on predicted health care costs of various individuals and groups, a method of premium setting called "experience rating." Commercial insurance companies found that they could offer premiums lower than Blue Cross–Blue Shield's community rate to customers expected to generate lower than average health care bills.

This form of competition created a dilemma for Blue Cross–Blue

Shield. If they stuck with community rating, they would be left with relatively costly customers, lose money, and eventually be driven out of business. If they kept community rating but boosted premiums to avoid losses, their remaining customers would move to private insurers. Faced with this choice, Blue Cross–Blue Shield dropped community rating and, like commercial insurance companies, began to relate premiums to expected costs. Thus competition among insurance companies resulted in the triumph of experience rating over community rating.

The importance of experience rating is growing as purchasers of insurance intensify their search for the lowest possible rates.[38] Insurers respond by trying to identify groups that have low costs and to offer insurance at the lowest possible premium. The inevitable result of such competition is that individuals or small groups with records of high costs and industries or members of occupations with high risks may be offered insurance only at rates several times the community average, or they may be denied coverage altogether.[39] People who belong to groups with a high incidence of certain diseases, including AIDS, or who have certain preexisting conditions find

38. Insurers can wholly ignore the loss experience of a particular group or can build actual losses into premiums in many ways. They can adjust rates quickly or slowly with respect to actual claims by the particular group or by some collection of groups of which the group is a member. Thus even community rating entails some recognition of the past losses of all the groups in the community taken together. At the opposite extreme, insurance companies may act as little more than bill payers if the premiums in one period are simply the losses of the preceding period. An increasing proportion of private companies have explicitly made insurance companies no more than bill payers by "self-insuring." Employers who self-insure pay whatever costs are incurred but hire another organization, often an insurance company, to process claims. The proportion of companies that self-insure has risen sharply, from an estimated 20 percent in 1980 to 66 percent in 1988. General Accounting Office, *Health Insurance: Cost Increases Lead to Coverage Limitations and Cost Shifting*, GAO/HRD-90-68 (May 1990), p. 21. By self-insuring, companies free themselves from restrictions that states impose on private insurance companies. The exemption comes from the Employee Retirement Income Security Act of 1974, which excused self-insured plans from state insurance regulation in order to subject them to a variety of federal regulations. See *Health Insurance and the Uninsured: Background Data and Analysis*, Committee Print, Subcommittee on Labor-Management Relations and Subcommittee on Labor Standards of House Committee on Education and Labor, Subcommittee on Health and the Environment of House Committee on Energy and Commerce, and Senate Special Committee on Aging, 100 Cong. 2 sess. (Government Printing Office, May 1988), pp. 77–84.

39. This problem figures prominently in popular criticisms of the current insurance system. See "The Crisis in Health Insurance," *Consumer Reports*, August 1990, pp. 533–49.

it difficult or impossible to buy coverage. Workers in hazardous occupations also find that insurance coverage is difficult or impossible to obtain.[40]

Adverse Selection

Imperfect information magnifies the large variations in insurance premiums that inevitably result from experience rating. Insurance companies know less, in certain dimensions, about how much health care their potential customers will use than the customers do. This asymmetry of information leads to adverse selection, the greater tendency of those who are more likely than average to use insurance to buy it. As a result, insurers will incur expenses higher than the average of all potentially insurable customers. To avoid losses, insurers set premiums higher than would be necessary to cover costs of a random sample of all potential customers.

To deal with this problem, insurance companies commonly refuse to insure companies with twenty-five or fewer employees unless the employees fill out health status questionnaires. If an employee admits to a potentially costly illness, such as diabetes or cancer, the insurer may exclude that employee from the plan (if state law permits) or deny coverage to the company unless the employer excludes that worker. The consequence of these practices is that small companies are finding health insurance increasingly costly or simply unavailable. As a result, more than half of all companies employing fewer than ten workers and more than 20 percent of firms employing ten to twenty-four workers did not offer insurance in 1984. Employees in companies with fewer than twenty-five workers formed almost half of the working uninsured.[41] This problem is less serious for large

40. "In an effort to avoid losses, many insurance carriers have quietly black-listed dozens of types of small businesses and professions. . . . While some health insurers have been accused of denying coverage to people in cities and occupations where the insurers contend the AIDS virus is most prevalent, the exclusions extend well beyond these groups. More than forty industries are listed as 'ineligible.' " Milt Freudenheim, "Health Insurers, to Reduce Losses, Blacklist Dozens of Occupations," New York Times, February 5, 1990, p. 1. The General Accounting Office lists twenty-nine industries that are ineligible for health insurance under selected insurer plans, including bars and taverns, commercial fishing, construction, foundries, grocery stores, hospitals and nursing homes, liquor stores, roofing companies, security guard companies, and trucking companies. See GAO, Health Insurance, p. 30.

41. GAO, Health Insurance, p. 26.

groups than for small ones, because the average costs of large groups deviate less around the average for a community than do the costs of small groups.[42]

Advances in understanding of genetic predisposition to particular illnesses promise to introduce new and serious problems. Genetic screening will enable insurers or employers to identify people susceptible to illness or vulnerable to identifiable workplace hazards. This capacity will reduce the problems of adverse selection but will create serious legal and ethical dilemmas. With such information in hand, self-insuring employers will have incentives to not hire workers who are likely to incur large medical expenses or to refuse to assign workers to activities that pose above-average risks. Insurance companies will be tempted to refuse coverage to companies, particularly those with few employees, who hire such workers.

Is Experience Rating Desirable?

The effects of experience rating and of adverse selection are inevitable under a competitive insurance market in which individuals

42. In extreme cases, adverse selection in a purely competitive market can make it impossible to sell insurance profitably, although the regulated sale of insurance would be profitable and socially beneficial. The following admittedly extreme example illustrates the point. Assume that six people are divided evenly between two groups, A and B. Members of group A have expected medical outlays of $1,000 per person when fully insured; members of group B have expected outlays of $2,000. Assume that administrative costs for selling insurance to six or fewer people total $1,200. (The assumption that administrative costs are fixed is admittedly extreme, but simplifies the example.) If everyone bought insurance, the average premium, including administrative costs, would be $1,700 (the average of the $1,000 cost per member of group A and the $2,000 cost per member of group B, plus administrative costs of $200 per person). If no members of group A are willing to pay $700 more than their expected outlays for insurance, then the minimum premium at which insurance can be sold profitably is $2,400 (the $2,000 cost for each member of group B, plus administrative costs of $1,200, which now are spread over only three people). If the three members of group B are willing to pay, say, $2,300, $2,500, and $3,000 for insurance, there is no price at which insurers can profitably offer coverage that anyone would be willing to buy. At a premium of $2,400, only two people will wish to buy insurance, but costs are $2,600, because the $1,200 in administrative costs must be recovered from only two policies. If the premium is raised to $2,600, only one person will buy insurance; but costs, including administration, are now $3,200. And at a price of $3,200, no one will demand insurance. This example illustrates a situation in which compulsory purchase of insurance might well raise social welfare.

and businesses are free to decide whether and from whom to buy insurance. They raise a crucial question: is experience rating desirable? On balance, the answer is no: the disadvantages of experience rating to the nation at large outweigh some very real benefits.

Medical costs of any group depend on a host of characteristics of the group, only some of which are subject to individual control or modification. Health outlays are correlated with characteristics such as sex, age, disabilities, and race, for example. If employers pay for health insurance, standard economic theory suggests that workers with relatively high expected health care costs, who therefore contribute greatly to groups' costs and experience-rated premiums, will receive less in money wages or other fringe benefits than would otherwise similar workers with low expected medical costs. The reasoning is that total compensation of workers will tend to equal the value of their marginal contribution to their employer's net revenues. If one component of compensation is relatively high for workers with given characteristics employed in jobs with given characteristics, other elements of compensation must be relatively low. If competition among firms fails to equalize total employment costs for workers of given skills in jobs with similar attributes, any variation in such costs attributable to health insurance premiums would show up in either product prices or the company's profits.

In many cases, social policy is well served by the variations in health insurance premiums that result from experience rating. The extra costs of health care for workers in hazardous occupations or for employers who do not maintain safe working conditions should be reflected in costs of doing business and should be borne by purchasers of these products through higher prices or by company owners through reduced profits. If companies locate in communities where health care is unusually expensive, the products of these companies should reflect the price of that locational decision, just as they should reflect higher than average land costs, wages, or state and local taxes. Price incentives for employers to minimize costs and wage differences to influence workers in job selections are essential in a market system, because they lead to efficient combinations of inputs. In addition, private insurance companies have used the incentives of experience rating to influence controllable personal behavior, for example, by offering nonsmokers lower rates or more generous insurance within groups. Employers use similar incentives to induce workers to seek care from preferred providers who have agreed to offer services at reduced rates.

In contrast, much of the variation in health care use is associated with characteristics that should not not affect other economic behavior. It is not clear why variations in health care costs associated with such characteristics should be reflected in the premiums paid by a particular employer whose work force consists of employees with unusual proportions of these characteristics and hence higher or lower than average health outlays. In particular, it is hard to see what positive social purpose is served when the higher than average health insurance premiums of groups that contain disproportionate numbers of older workers, physically disabled workers, African Americans, women, or gay men lead to higher prices for purchasers of the goods or services produced by such groups, to lower profits for employers who hire such workers, or to reduced wages for other workers employed in such companies. Such effects can be avoided if members of groups with high health costs are paid lower money wages or given fewer or less costly fringe benefits other than health care. But laws have been enacted explicitly to prohibit wage or other discrimination based on age, sex, race, or disability.

This line of argument seems to justify the continuation of experience rating only if it is confined to variations in health expenses not associated with uncontrollable characteristics. Under such a policy, insurance companies would be permitted to vary premiums based on workplace conditions or controllable personal behaviors for a hypothetical population with average age, race, sex, and disability composition. Such a system would be difficult or impossible to sustain in practice. Insurers would face powerful incentives to offer good service and market aggressively to the low-cost groups and to provide bad service and indifferent marketing to high-cost groups. These incentives might perhaps be suppressed by regulation. For example, customers could be randomly assigned to insurers and service could be monitored. But such measures would be so intrusive that they would eliminate most of the other advantages of competition. Because free competition among insurance companies is unimaginable without widespread experience rating, the disadvantages of experience rating argue for moving away from a system of private

competitive insurance and must be weighed along with other consid-
erations in deciding whether to retain private health insurance.

A Dilemma

The argument advanced in this chapter may be summarized in
four propositions. First, insurance creates incentives for patients to
demand and for physicians to provide health care that is expensive
relative to benefits. Second, powerful forces are reducing the capacity
of insurance to serve as many people in the future as it has in the
past. Third, any system of health insurance that rests on many
separate, privately negotiated contracts and that involves multiple
channels of payment to providers for each patient will have major
advantages, but these advantages will be purchased at enormous
administrative cost. Fourth, multiple channels of payment inherent
in the current U.S. financing system make it difficult or impossible to
reduce the amount of low-benefit, high-cost care. These propositions
rest on certain identifiable characteristics of the U.S. system, described in the next chapter.

These propositions add up to a dilemma. The United States can
continue its current financing system without major change. But if
it does so, strong forces will act to reduce the number of people with
health insurance and to continue driving up the amount spent on
low-benefit care. Or it can contemplate major changes in that system.

CHAPTER THREE

Organization and Financing

REFORMS OF health care financing should rest on an understanding of why costs have been rising, how current financing arrangements work, and how well they are operating. Measures to slow the growth of health care spending should rest on an accurate reading of the causes of rising outlays. Similarly, measures to extend health insurance coverage to the uninsured should reflect an understanding of private and public coverage and the incentives that govern private decisions about health insurance.

Health Care Expenditures

Real health care spending was more than nine times as high in 1990 as in 1950 (table 3-1). Part of this increase simply reflects population growth, but real per capita spending, which grew at an annual average of 4.4 percent, more than quintupled.[1] Because national output per capita rose 98 percent, the share devoted to health care nearly tripled, from 4.8 percent of net national product to 13.7 percent.

1. Here and elsewhere nominal expenditures at different dates and in different countries are deflated by the deflator for gross national or gross domestic product. The reasons I use broad-based price indices rather than estimates of health care prices are set forth more fully below in this chapter and in appendix A of chapter 4.

Table 3–1. *Growth in U.S. Health Care Spending, Selected Years, 1950–90*

Year	Outlays (billions of 1990 constant dollars)[a]	Outlays (percent of NNP)[a]	Per capita outlays (1990 dollars)	Annual growth in period (percent of per capita outlays)
1950	69.9	4.8	459	. . .
1960	115.3	5.9	638	3.3
1970	232.9	8.0	1,136	5.9
1980	382.2	10.3	1,678	4.0
1988	585.3	12.4	2,376	4.4
1990	671.0	13.7	2,604	4.7

Sources: Katharine R. Levit and others, "National Health Care Spending, 1989," *Health Affairs*, vol. 10 (Spring 1991), pp. 117–30; Katharine R. Levit, Mark S. Freeland, and Daniel R. Waldo, "National Health Care Spending Trends, 1988," *Health Affairs*, vol. 9 (Summer 1990), pp. 171–84; and Barbara S. Cooper, Nancy L. Worthington, and Mary F. McGee, "Compendium of National Health Expenditure Data," DHEW pub. (SSA) 76-11927 (Social Security Administration, January 1976), p. 4.
a. Deflated using GNP deflator.

Causes of Rising Expenditures

Five factors have contributed to the increase in per capita spending: the extension of third-party payment through private insurance and public programs, which encourages demand for health care by reducing the cost at time of illness; an apparent increase in the relative price of medical services; the aging of the American population, which will continue to boost medical spending for at least half a century; malpractice, which has boosted costs of medical practice and is alleged to have caused physicians to render unnecessary care from fear of litigation; and a technological revolution, which has remade medical science in a generation. Of these factors, the importance of all but technological change has been greatly exaggerated.[2]

FINANCING. The spread of private insurance for hospital and physician expenses, especially during the 1950s and 1960s, reduced the price of care to patients at time of illness and increased demand for care. The proportion of hospital bills paid out-of-pocket by individuals fell from 30 percent in 1950 to 9 percent in 1970.[3] Research has

2. This section rests critically on the contributions William B. Schwartz has made to the analysis of rising health costs and on ideas he has conveyed in personal conversations.
3. Office of National Cost Estimates, "National Health Expenditures, 1988," *Health Care Financing Review*, vol. 11 (Summer 1990), p. 27; and Barbara S. Cooper, Nancy L. Worthington, and Mary F. McGee, "Compendium of National Health Ex-

indicated that the quantity of health care demanded responds to the price people face. A 10 percent decrease in price will boost health care expenditures by 1 to 2 percent.[4] The proportion of total health spending paid by individuals fell from 65 percent to 27 percent between 1950 and 1983. If the price of health care had not risen relative to other goods, this drop in price would be expected to increase spending on health care 8 to 16 percent. In fact, per capita health care spending rose 327 percent. Clearly, the simple drop in the price of health care because of the extension of insurance cannot explain any significant part of the growth of spending.

This simple approach conceals as much as it reveals. First, the extension of health insurance helped to create the economic climate in which the technological innovations alluded to above could be implemented.[5] Second, the extension of insurance significantly increased the likelihood that people would seek medical care, but had a much smaller effect on expenditures per episode of care.[6] Third, the effect of insurance on demand varies widely from person to person and from service to service because the complex system of deductibles, copayments, and limits on patient financial liability creates different prices for patients at different times of the year and for different medical procedures, depending on whether patients have spent enough to escape deductibles or other forms of cost sharing.

None of these qualifications, however, disturbs the fundamental conclusion that while the spread of insurance contributed to the rise of health care spending in the United States, the direct effect was relatively small. In particular, health care spending has grown at

penditure Data," DHEW pub. (SSA) 76-11927 (Social Security Administration, January 1976), p. 91.

4. Willard G. Manning and others, *Health Insurance and the Demand for Medical Care: Evidence from a Randomized Experiment* (Rand Corporation, 1988). Also see Joseph P. Newhouse and others, "Some Interim Results from a Controlled Trial of Cost Sharing in Health Insurance," *New England Journal of Medicine*, December 17, 1981, pp. 1501–07.

5. Joseph P. Newhouse, "The Structure of Health Insurance and the Erosion of Competition in the Medical Marketplace," in Warren Greenberg, ed., *Competition in the Health Care Sector: Past, Present, and Future* (Germantown, Md.: Aspen Systems Corp., 1978), pp. 270–87; and Newhouse, "Has the Erosion of the Medical Marketplace Ended?" *Journal of Health Politics, Policy, and Law*, vol. 13 (Summer 1988), pp. 263–77.

6. Emmett B. Keeler and John E. Rolph, "The Demand for Episodes of Treatment in the Health Insurance Experiment," *Journal of Health Economics*, vol. 7 (December 1988), pp. 337–68; and Emmett B. Keeler, Willard G. Manning, and Kenneth B. Wells, "The Demand for Episodes of Mental Health Services," *Journal of Health Economics*, vol. 7 (December 1988), pp. 369–92.

rates far greater than per capita national output since 1950, although growth accelerated somewhat during the 1960s, when medicare and medicaid were enacted.

RELATIVE PRICE INCREASE. According to official statistics, the relative price of health care services has increased dramatically.[7] Some increase in the relative price of medical care almost certainly has occurred because the compensation of hospital employees has risen sharply relative to the average pay in other occupations. Between mid-1963 and 1989, pay of head nurses rose 75.9 percent; nurse supervisors, 62.5 percent; nursing instructors, 50 percent; medical records administrators, 44.5 percent; licensed practical nurses, 44.1 percent; physical therapists, 35.2 percent; radiographers, 33.5 percent; dieticians, 20.9 percent; and medical social workers, 11.8 percent.[8] Meanwhile, average earnings rose 7.0 percent in manufacturing and fell 0.58 percent in construction and 25.7 percent in retail trade.

Aside from rising relative wages, it is difficult to tell whether the price of medical care has risen or fallen and, if so, by how much.[9] The most serious problem is that the price of medical care fails to meet the necessary condition of any price index, that it measure the price of the *same product* over time, or, when quality changes, that it adjusts for quality change. As Joseph Newhouse remarked:

> From artificial hips, to noninvasive diagnostic machines, to improved mortality rates for childhood leukemias, to TPA [tissue plasminogen activator] for heart attacks, we are not pricing a product whose characteristics do not change. Because a correction is rarely made for these improvements, part of what we term a

7. If health care prices as officially measured had risen at the same rate as the overall consumer price index between 1970 and 1990, health prices would have been 42 percent lower than they actually were. For reasons indicated below, this comparison is not meaningful.

8. Department of Labor, Bureau of Labor Statistics, "Industry Wage Survey: Hospitals, United States and Selected Metropolitan Areas, March 1989," Summary 90-3 (April 1990); and BLS, "Industry Wage Survey: Hospitals, Mid-1963," Bulletin 1409 (June 1964).

9. The following points are taken from Joseph P. Newhouse, "Measuring Medical Prices and Understanding Their Effects: The Baxter Foundation Prize Address," *Journal of Health Administration Education*, vol. 7 (Winter 1989), pp. 19–26. For an examination of additional problems, see appendix A of chapter 4.

price increase is instead improved quality. How much the improved quality is worth is a difficult issue, but the current index usually pretends it is not worth anything and that the additional expenditure is pure inflation.[10]

The price of hospital services in official statistics is the price of one day in a hospital and does not incorporate any recognition of the increased flow of real services per day, which has contributed to reduced average lengths of stay. From 1971 to 1986 the ratio of hospital employees to patients rose from 2.72 to 3.92.[11] Yet these changes in the actual service rendered are not captured in official statistics.[12]

In addition, the health care component of the consumer price index reflects only out-of-pocket outlays by households. Hence movements in the price index are determined not by the total price of care, but by the fraction of that cost that consumers bear. Thus, although expenditures on hospital services are nearly twice as large as those on physicians and nearly eight times those on dentists, the CPI weights the price of physicians' services more heavily than the price of hospital services and the price of dentists' services about as heavily. And the most recent revision of the CPI reduced the weight of medical care in the overall index by more than 20 percent, despite the continuing increase in total medical costs, because out-of-pocket payments by households represented a diminishing share of total consumption.[13]

AGING.   An increase in the average age of the population boosts costs of health care because per capita spending on the elderly is higher than that on the young. Per capita health care spending in 1987 was $745 for people under age 19, $1,535 for people aged 19 through 64, $5,360 for people aged 65 and over, and $9,178 for people aged 85 or

10. Newhouse, "Measuring Medical Prices," p. 24.
11. See Department of Health and Human Services, National Center for Health Statistics, *Health, United States, 1988,* DHSS pub. (PHS) 89-1232 (DHHS, 1989), p. 158.
12. This problem is not unique to health care. For example, in measures of the price of services of financial institutions, no account is taken of the convenience resulting from the advent of automatic teller machines.
13. Newhouse, "Measuring Medical Prices," p. 24.

Figure 3–1. *Elderly Population in the United States, Selected Years, 1950–2040*

Millions (log scale)

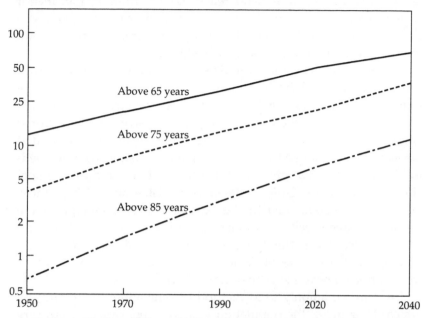

Sources: Bureau of the Census, "Estimates of the Population of the United States, by Single Years of Age, Color and Sex, 1900 to 1959," *Current Population Reports*, series P-25, no. 311 (Department of Commerce, 1965); Bureau of the Census, *Statistical Abstract of the United States: 1990*, 110th ed. (Department of Commerce, 1990), p. 37, table 41; and Department of Health and Human Services, "Social Security Area Population Projections: 1989," SSA pub. 11-11552 (June 1989), pp. 33–35.

over.[14] The population of the United States is growing older and will continue to do so well into the next century (see figure 3-1) Because the consumption of health care rises sharply with age, this demographic trend pushes up health care spending.

Aging of the U.S. population will certainly increase health care spending, but how much is not clear. The uncertainty arises because the population will be aging for two distinct reasons. First, a drop in birth rates means that the proportion of the population that is elderly will rise as large age cohorts, most notably the baby boom generation

14. Daniel R. Waldo and others, "Health Expenditures by Age Group, 1977 and 1987," *Health Care Financing Review*, vol. 10 (Summer 1989), pp. 116–18. Waldo and his coauthors consider outlays on hospitals, physician services, and nursing homes.

born from 1945 through 1965, become elderly. This trend unambiguously raises per capita spending. It would occur even if life expectancies were unchanged. In addition, however, life expectancies have been rising among those who reach age 65, from 15.1 years for women who reached age 65 in 1950, to 19.0 years in 1990 and a projected 21.8 years in 2050.[15] This second factor is also pushing up the fraction of the population that is elderly.

Increased life expectancy would be associated with reduced health care spending if such health influences as improved diet or exercise reduced the frequency of long, costly, degenerative illnesses and people increasingly died after brief, inexpensive illnesses. But it would be associated with increased health care spending if extended life expectancy resulted from either behavioral changes or new medical interventions that prevented death but did not reduce age-specific rates of illness. Little evidence is available on which of these factors has predominated in the past or will predominate in the future, but age-specific disability rates have risen slightly in the United States.[16] This trend suggests that medical advances are extending the lives of people who would have died in earlier times from various illnesses that they now survive.

The most commonly used method of estimating the amount by which the aging of the population will boost per capita health care spending is to weight the older age groups' higher health care spending by their rising relative size in the population.[17] According to this method, the aging of the U.S. population will boost per capita health care spending relative to that in 1990 by 12 percent in 2020 and by 23 percent in 2040.

Unless most of the increase in life expectancy came from extending the lives of the disabled, this estimate is almost certainly an exaggera-

15. Department of Health and Human Services, "Social Security Area Population Projections: 1989," Actuarial Study 105, June 1989, p. 14.

16. Kyriakos S. Markides, "Trends in the Health of the Elderly in Western Societies," paper prepared for a conference on Work, Age, and Social Security, sponsored by the Foundation for International Studies on Social Securities, June 13–15, 1990. Markides finds that the age-adjusted rate of disability is increasing in the United States and the United Kingdom and is falling in Sweden.

17. In symbols, the proportional increase in health care spending is estimated as $[\Sigma\, H_{i0}W_{it} / \Sigma\, H_{i0}W_{i0}] - 1$, where the subscript i refers to the various age groups; the subscripts t and 0 refer, respectively, to some future date and the current time; H refers to per capita health care spending; and W is the population share.

tion of the contribution of aging.[18] A major reason for the rise in health care spending with age is the large expenditure in the year or two just before death. As life expectancies rise, the proportion of each cohort expected to die in any given year will fall, thus tending to reduce age-specific health expenditures. To be sure, new medical procedures may contribute to this extension of life expectancy; but the increase in outlays associated with such interventions is a function of scientific advances, not of demographic trends.

MALPRACTICE LITIGATION. Patients who suffer adverse medical outcomes because of negligence by physicians, hospitals, or other medical providers are legally entitled to compensation for their losses. Many blame malpractice litigation for a large part of increased medical expenditures. Premiums add directly to practice costs of physicians and to overhead costs of hospitals. Of possibly greater importance, it is alleged that fear of litigation causes providers to practice "defensive medicine"—medically unnecessary tests and other services that would not be carried out if the threat of being sued were not present.

Close students of medical malpractice litigation and insurance argue that malpractice insurance and litigation cannot add more than marginally to total medical spending and that much of what is called defensive medicine provides some medical benefits. Medical malpractice insurance premiums of physicians in 1989 totaled about 3.4 percent of physician income and 0.8 percent of personal medical spending.[19] Hospital malpractice insurance adds to these amounts, but does not change the fact that even if these premiums were zero at some time in the past, they cannot directly account for much of the growth of health care spending.

The allegation that medical practice is distorted by fear of litigation is more serious. While the behavior of some physicians, particularly

18. Medical expenditures on the disabled are about five times larger than those on persons without disabilities. Dorothy P. Rice and Mitchell LaPlante, "Costs of Chronic Comorbidity," paper prepared for the 1988 annual meeting of the American Public Health Association.

19. Frank A. Sloan, Randall R. Bovbjerg, and Penny Githens, *Insuring Medical Malpractice* (Oxford University Press, forthcoming). Patricia M. Danzon reported that medical malpractice insurance premiums of physicians and hospitals totaled 1.1 percent of total health expenditures in 1975 and 0.74 percent in 1982. See *Medical Malpractice: Theory, Evidence, and Public Policy* (Harvard University Press, 1985), pp. 186–87.

in some specialties, may be distorted by these fears, a survey of physicians indicated that possible malpractice litigation ranked fourth in a list of seven influences on standards of care, below continuing medical education, medical journals, and peer relations.[20] Since the usual defense in malpractice litigation is that the physician followed standard practices, the failure to follow procedures that have not been shown to provide any clear benefit is not a culpable act. Juries are sometimes known to abandon this legal doctrine, however, especially when the plaintiff is poor or elicits sympathy, a possibility of which physicians are acutely aware. More positively, services provided under the guise of defensive medicine provide information of some value in planning treatment as well as protection against adverse outcomes.

Although the malpractice system is not the force in boosting total health care spending that many suppose, the system is seriously deficient because it fails to perform its two major functions: to compensate victims of medical negligence and to penalize inept providers, thereby encouraging them to do better or to leave medicine.

The current system of adversary litigation provides compensation to only a minuscule fraction of those who suffer injury because of medical negligence—not more than 6.25 percent and possibly fewer than 1 percent, according to a recent study of medical malpractice in New York. It provides no compensation to most victims of relatively minor injuries or to most victims of even severe injuries who are over age 65.[21] Neither type of case is profitable to litigate because damages for lost earnings or for pain and suffering are likely to be small. Less than half of settlements paid to the small fraction of successful litigants ends up in the hands of those who suffered injury. The rest is absorbed by trial costs, including lawyers' fees, which often reach one-third of the settlement, and by administrative expenses associated with malpractice insurance.

Malpractice insurance mutes incentives that the tort system creates for health care providers to furnish standard care. It does so because insurance shifts much of the financial risk from providers to the insurers, and because virtually all physicians practicing a given

20. *Patients, Doctors, and Lawyers: Medical Injury, Malpractice Litigation, and Patient Compensation in New York: The Report of the Harvard Medical Practice Study to The State of New York* (Harvard Medical Practice Study, 1990), p. 9-25.

21. *Patients, Doctors, and Lawyers*, pp. 7-39, 7-40, 9-25.

specialty in a given area face the same premium, whether they have been sued successfully or not. Some incentives remain because suits damage a physician's reputation, take time to defend, and are quite unpleasant. Furthermore, the small minority of repeat offenders may be denied coverage by regular sellers of malpractice insurance and be forced to seek coverage from other providers at much higher rates.

The failure of insurers to vary premiums based on the loss experience of physicians is surprising, because it appears that insurers could increase profits if they did so.[22] Experience rating would have some effect on the incentives most physicians face, but many years often elapse between negligent medical practices and ultimate settlement in court. The delays arise not only because judicial proceedings are lengthy, but also because many injuries are not immediately and fully apparent. Delays are particularly frequent in the case of obstetric malpractice that results in birth defects, the full consequences of which may not be clear until the child is several years old. Indeed, determination of whether a physician's or a hospital's behavior in a particular case deviated sufficiently from standard practice to be characterized as malpractice is often a very close call.[23] These factors taken together mean that it would be many years before an insurer could fairly conclude that a particular physician deserved to be charged higher than average premiums. By the time such pricing could be sustained, the genuinely incompetent physician would have been negligent many times. Furthermore, such surcharges would apply to only the small fraction of malpractice that is currently litigated and results in a court settlement. In short, since many instances of malpractice occur for each one that ever appears in the courts or results in settlement, incentives confronting providers to practice

22. Sufficient information is available for insurance companies to experience rate either individual physicians or groups of physicians practicing through hospitals. See Frank A. Sloan and Mahmud Hassan, "Equity and Accuracy in Medical Malpractice Insurance Pricing," *Journal of Health Economics*, vol. 9 (November 1990), pp. 289–319.

23. Many medical procedures are inherently risky even if well executed. The course of action in many situations is a matter of judgment about which competent physicians disagree. Confronted with a hypothetical pregnancy and delivery that resulted in birth defects, one obstetrician said of the behavior attributed to the delivering physician: "I would say there are significant ways here to avoid what happened. And to me, when you can avoid a problem, you're negligent." Another obstetrician remarked: "Perhaps it's bad judgment, but I don't think it was neglect." Yet another commented: "I don't think it was a well managed case, [but] I don't think negligence has any bearing at all." *Patients, Doctors, and Lawyers*, pp. 9-55, 9-56.

standard medicine and avoid malpractice litigation may be of the wrong kind, but they are not too strong.

TECHNOLOGY. More than any other factor, the proliferation of medical technology explains the growth of health care spending. The development of medical technology affects outlays in two distinct ways: by adding to the menu of feasible treatments and by reducing the invasiveness of existing interventions, thereby increasing the number of patients who stand to enjoy net gains from diagnosis or treatment.

The range of beneficial diagnostic and therapeutic interventions has expanded rapidly and without interruption for several decades. They include bypass surgery and balloon angioplasty to open partially blocked coronary arteries; transplants for failed livers, eyes, and hearts; artificial knees and hips; implants to regulate heart rhythms and improve hearing; dialysis to replace failed kidneys; microsurgery and other innovations that spare patients hospitalization for corneal transplants, hernia repairs, and gall bladder removal; and bone marrow transplants to treat certain forms of cancer and anemia. These and dozens of other diagnostic and therapeutic procedures came into existence within the lifetimes of most Americans alive today.

Other advances, such as antibiotics, which seem to reduce medical costs by treating common diseases at much lower cost than was possible with past methods of care, in fact have greatly added to total medical spending in two ways. First, since death from infectious disease is relatively inexpensive and comparatively painless—pneumonia was long known as "the widow's friend"—those spared death by antibiotics have an increased chance of succumbing later to more protracted, painful, and costly illnesses, such as cancer or Alzheimer's disease. Second, antibiotics are an essential part of standard protocols for treating cancer. Cytotoxic drugs frequently undermine natural defenses against infection and can be used only if artificial barriers to infection are created. Thus antibiotics enable costly therapies that would be lethal without them.

In other cases, technological advances enable physicians to gather information that in the past would have required painful or dangerous interventions. CT scanners and magnetic resonance imaging, for example, supply information noninvasively about the functioning of internal organs and the character and location of lesions that once required exploratory surgery or other invasive procedures. Because the new procedures are without significant risk, the savings from reduced surgery are spent many times over on a vastly increased number of tests.

The pace of scientific innovation in medical diagnosis and treatment promises to continue and quite possibly to accelerate. In the wake of CT scanning and magnetic resonance imaging comes positron emission tomography. Proton-beam accelerators promise increased radiation dosage to cancers with reduced damage to surrounding tissues at a total facility cost of $60 million.[24] Monoclonal antibodies to treat cancer are tailor-made for each patient. Cochlear implants promise to aid the hearing of many of the roughly 21 million deaf people in the United States. And genetic and molecular research holds the promise of individualized therapies to treat or prevent inherited diseases such as cystic fibrosis, diabetes, and various forms of cancer.

Low-Benefit, High-Cost Care

Most common medical procedures have never been subject to controlled evaluation to determine in which cases the procedures produce expected benefits and whether alternative approaches might be superior. Some analysts hold that simply by eliminating care that produces little or no benefit, health care expenditures could be cut as much as 30 percent and that service could be extended and improved at no increase in cost.[25]

Partly because of a hope that large savings can be achieved, the federal government is sponsoring research to examine the effectiveness of various medical interventions. Initial research is focusing on

24. "Beam of Hope: A Proton Accelerator Is the Most Costly Medicine Yet," *Scientific American*, vol. 263 (December 1990), pp. 24–25.

25. Robert H. Brook and Mary E. Vaiana, *Appropriateness of Care: A Chart Book*, report prepared for George Washington University, National Health Policy Forum (Washington, June 1989). According to John E. Wennberg, "Outcomes research holds out hope for those who want to believe that full entitlement to effective health care is attainable within the limits of our national willingness to fund medical care. . . . I want to suggest [that] . . . the proportion of the gross national product now invested in health care may exceed the proportion required to fund fully the caring and effective services that patients want." "Outcomes Research, Cost Containment, and the Fear of Health Care Rationing," *New England Journal of Medicine*, October 25, 1990, pp. 1202–04.

four common health problems and associated therapies: enlarged prostates among older men, low back pain, myocardial infarction ("heart attacks"), and cataracts. Subsequent research will address other illnesses. Appropriations for this research rose from $5.9 million in 1989 to $32 million in 1990 and are certain to rise much more.[26]

Behind the support for this research lies not only the hope that large savings will result from the elimination of medically unnecessary diagnosis and treatment, but also the realization that improved knowledge can improve the quality of medical care.[27] Those who think that efficacy studies will result in large savings cite the wide variations in the rates at which common procedures are performed and the high proportion of certain procedures performed when they are not medically indicated.[28]

Although large gross savings may result, they are not likely to materially slow the growth of overall health care spending for three distinct reasons. First, even though therapies used may sometimes be inappropriate, the symptoms that occasioned therapy typically call for some other form of possibly less costly treatment. The net saving is not the cost of the inappropriate therapy, but the difference between that cost and the alternative that must be provided. Second, effectiveness research is often complex and time consuming. Effectiveness can be measured in many ways, such as decrease in mortality over a variety of periods, alleviation of pain, or facilitation of mobility. Clear-cut results will sometimes emerge, but many studies will reveal conflicts in which a particular therapy is superior in some respects and inferior in others. Clear information on effects of therapy, while useful, will often justify diverse decisions based on each patient's values and preferences. Furthermore, the results of such studies will become available slowly over a number of years. At the same time, large numbers of new medical devices and procedures will come into use, most of which will tend to drive up overall

26. Janet Ochs Wiener, ed., "Technology Assessment's Winding Road," *Medicine and Health*, April 23, 1990.

27. Arnold M. Epstein, "Sounding Board: The Outcomes Movement—Will It Get Us Where We Want to Go?" *New England Journal of Medicine*, July 26, 1990, pp. 266–69.

28. John E. Wennberg and Alan Gittelsohn, "Variations in Medical Care among Small Areas," *Scientific American*, vol. 246 (April 1982), pp. 120–34; and Mark R. Chassin and others, "Does Appropriate Use Explain Geographic Variations in the Use of Health Care Services?" *Journal of the American Medical Association*, November 13, 1987, pp. 2533–37.

Table 3–2. *Concentration of Health Care Outlays, Selected Countries and Selected Years, 1928–88*
Percent

Proportion of population ranked by health outlays	U.S. population			Medicare	France	Canada (elderly)	
	1928	1970	1980	1982	1980–81	1972	1972–88
Top 1 percent	n.a.	26	29	20	n.a.	n.a.	n.a.
Top 5 percent	52	50	55	54	64	65	28
Top 10 percent	n.a.	66	70	75[a]	74	79	44
Top 30 percent	93	88	90	n.a.	92	n.a.	n.a.
Top 50 percent	n.a.	96	96	n.a.	99	100	93

Sources: U.S. population, Marc L. Berk, Alan C. Monheit, and Michael M. Hagan, "How the U.S. Spent Its Health Care Dollar: 1929–80," *Health Affairs*, vol. 7 (Fall 1988), p. 50; medicare and France, Organization for Economic Cooperation and Development, *Financing and Delivering Health Care: A Comparative Analysis of OECD Countries* (Paris, 1987), pp. 21–22; and Canada, Noralou P. Roos, Evelyn Shapiro, and Robert Tate, "Does A Small Majority of Elderly Account for a Majority of Health Care Expenditures?: A Sixteen-year Perspective," *Milbank Quarterly*, vol. 67, supp. 2, pt.2 (1989), p. 353.
n.a. Not available.
a. Calculated from data for 8.8 percent and 11 percent.

costs. Third, some efficacy studies will identify procedures that are underused, on which expenditures should be increased.

The best that can be expected in the way of cost control from effectiveness research is likely to be some savings, gradually realized over a period when forces driving up costs continue to operate. Even if nothing is saved, however, effectiveness research will have amply repaid its cost if it leads to improved accuracy of medical and surgical therapy.

Concentration of Health Care Outlays

Each year a small proportion of the population accounts for the majority of health care outlays (table 3-2). Five percent of the population accounts for more than half of all health care outlays in any given year. One percent of the population spends more than one-fourth of all health care outlays. Half of the population spends little on health care. This pattern holds not only for the elderly but for the general population as well, and it shows up not only in the United States but in France and Canada. Data for other countries would almost certainly look generally the same.

These patterns might arise because only a small proportion of the population became ill each year even if everyone used health care identically over the long run. Even over a period as long as sixteen years, however, a minority of the population uses most health care, and the majority uses little.

Some rough arithmetic indicates the magnitudes involved. According to table 3-2, per capita outlays on the part of the population making greatest use of health care were twenty-nine times the national average for the top 1 percent and eleven times for the top 5 percent in 1980. Given per capita health spending in 1990 of approximately $2,500, per capita outlays on health care for the most costly 1 percent and 5 percent of the population averaged $72,500 and $27,500, respectively.

The concentration of health care outlays creates enormous incentives for private insurers to try to identify customers likely to be heavy users. Insurers who can keep the number of high-cost customers to a minimum can make good profits while keeping premiums low. Failure to screen out the high-cost customers can be financially calamitous.

Implications

The fact that technological change has been and will remain the dominant explanation of rising health care outlays is both good news and bad. It is good news because improved technology means that much of the increase in the cost of care has been associated with beneficial treatments. It is bad news because the potential for technological change is unlimited, while the inflationary effects of the other cost factors are not only small but limited. Even if all of the inflation arising from fear of malpractice litigation, the extension of insurance, and care providing negligible benefits could somehow be eliminated, the dominant underlying force responsible for rising medical outlays—technological advances—would remain.[29]

The facts presented above lead to my central conclusion about cost control. Curtailment of the generosity of insurance (for example, through increased cost sharing), reform of the malpractice system,

29. William B. Schwartz, "The Inevitable Failure of Current Cost-Containment Strategies: Why They Can Provide Only Temporary Relief," *Journal of the American Medical Association*, January 9, 1987, pp. 220–24. See also Henry J. Aaron and William B. Schwartz, "Rationing Health Care: The Choice before Us," *Science*, January 26, 1990, pp. 418–22.

and effectiveness analysis cannot reduce the growth in health care spending on a sustained basis. A sustained reduction would require the curtailment of care that is beneficial but is deemed to be excessively costly, in other words, the rationing of health care.

This conclusion poses the crucial question that all who would slow growth of spending on health care must confront: is there an ethically supportable and politically sustainable way to ration care? Without such a mechanism, spending on low-benefit, high-cost care will continue to rise as technological advances cause a proliferation of services. Even with such a mechanism, total health care spending is likely to continue rising, in absolute terms and as a fraction of national product. But if the administration of increased outlays is efficient and equitable, the added spending would command popular support. The concentration of expenditures on a few patients underscores the fact that any measures that successfully reduce the rate of growth of spending on health care must eventually affect outlays on high-cost episodes. Successful cost control will have to center on care associated with hospitalizations or with costly outpatient treatment for chronic illnesses. In short, successful cost control will require rationing of services to the very ill.

Sources of Payment

Six out of seven Americans have health insurance, in the sense that someone else is contractually or legally obligated to pay for their medical care.[30] Some receive insurance through employment; some are covered by employer-sponsored plans; some buy insurance for themselves; and some receive it through a government program. The ways in which such payments are arranged differ enormously. The differences in coverage are central to the current debate about health care financing. What is health insurance? Who has it? Why does it matter?

30. Someone other than the patient often pays for care for the uninsured, as well. Physicians provide charity care and hospitals incur unreimbursed expenses. In both cases, the costs are normally passed on to other payers. See Frank A. Sloan, James F. Blumstein, and James M. Perrin, *Uncompensated Hospital Care: Rights and Responsibilities* (Johns Hopkins University Press, 1986).

Private Insurance

Two-thirds of Americans under age 65 and nearly three-fourths of employees are covered by employer-sponsored plans.[31] Employees of small companies are less likely than employees of large companies to have health insurance, for reasons noted in chapter 2. Approximately 14 million people under age 65 are covered by insurance bought by individuals.[32]

The range of protection from acute-care health insurance varies enormously. Because each private insurance plan has its own limits and many employers offer more than one plan, the American population is covered by a bewildering variety of health insurance policies (table 3-3). Almost all plans cover hospitalization and associated physicians' services, although benefits vary widely; for example, preexisting conditions may be uninsured. Some health maintenance organizations (HMOs) and indemnity insurance plans provide virtually unlimited hospital and physicians' benefits. Public coverage under medicaid is comprehensive in some states but highly restricted in others.[33] Plans differ in the amounts they will pay physicians; whether physicians may bill patients for charges in addition to those covered by insurance; the proportion of the premium that employees must pay for their own or their family's coverage; and whether coverage extends to nursing homes, home health care, inpatient mental health benefits, outpatient mental health benefits, treatment of alcohol and other drug abuse, and the services of such providers as podiatrists, chiropractors, optometrists, and Christian Science practitioners. Moreover, insurance coverage changes, often in rather fundamental ways, for many of those who change jobs or move from one community to another.

Recent innovations in private insurance are designed to lower

31. Among employees, 56 percent are covered in their own right. An additional 17 percent are covered as dependents of other workers. Employee Benefit Research Institute, *Issue Brief*, no. 104 (Washington, July 1990).

32. An additional 10.5 million people aged 65 and above also buy individual plans, usually as a supplement to medicare. EBRI, *Issue Brief*, no. 104.

33. Lousiana pays for only ten days of hospitalization a year and ten inpatient physician visits a year. Several other medicaid programs have similar, if somewhat less stringent, limits. Most states have no limits on hospitalization or physician visits. *Medicaid Source Book: Background Data and Analysis*, Committee Print, Subcommittee on Health and the Environment of the House Committee on Energy and Commerce, 100 Cong. 2 sess. (Government Printing Office, 1988), tables III-3, III-4.

Table 3–3. *Limits on Coverage among Health Insurance Plans*

Limit	Percent of employer-sponsored plans[a]	Medicare[b]	Medicaid[b]
Particular benefits			
Hospitalization and medical care	100	Yes	Yes[c]
Dental care	87	No	Varies[c]
Physical examinations	71	Yes	Yes[c]
Vision care	21	No	Varies[c]
Separate prescription drug plan	12	No	No
Deductible for covered services			
$50 or less	6	Part A: first day	No deductible
$100	47	in hospital,	
$150	20	$628; part B:	
$200	20	first day in	
More than $200	7	hospital, $100	
Lifetime limits on benefits for covered services			
Under $250,000	3	90 days of	No limit
$250,000	11	hospitalization;[d]	
$250,000–$750,000	16	no limit on	
$1 million and over	44	physician	
No maximum	26	services	
Maximum patient expense for covered services			
$500 or less	23	No maximum	0
$501–999	12		
$1,000–$2,000	36		
Over $2,000	4		
No provision	17		
Total monthly premiums			
Individual			
Under $50	7	$31.90	0
$50–69	35		
$70–89	34		
$90–119	19		
$120 or over	5		
Family			
Under $130	6		
$130–189	40		
$190–219	19		
$220–280	27		
Over $280	8		

Source: *Health Insurance and the Uninsured: Background Data and Analysis,* Committee Print, Subcommittee on Labor-Management Relations and Subcommittee on Labor Standards of House Committee on Education and Labor, Subcommittee on Health and the Environment of House Committee on Energy and Commerce, and Senate Special Committee on Aging, 100 Cong. 2 sess. (Government Printing Office, May 1988), tables 2.6, 2.9, 2.11, 2.12 and charts 2.3, 2.5.

a. From data published in 1987.

b. As of 1991.

c. Limits on benefits vary from state to state.

d. Part A pays the full cost of up to sixty days of hospitalization per illness and three-fourths of the cost of the next thirty days per illness after the patient has paid a deductible ($628 in 1991).

premiums. Approximately 32.5 million people receive care from HMOs.[34] Preferred provider organizations, which combine limits on cost sharing with restricted choice of providers, were available to 21 percent of workers in 1989.[35] Such plans require less cost sharing than plans that permit patients a free choice of providers. A rapidly growing proportion of conventional health insurance plans provide for managed care.[36] However, typical strategies of managed care are usually viewed as ineffective in holding down costs.[37]

Outlay Trends

Hospital spending accounted for nearly half of personal health care outlays in 1989, and hospitals and physicians taken together accounted for two-thirds (table 3-4). The share of the health care dollar flowing to hospitals rose gradually from 1960 until 1980 and has declined slightly since, while physicians have claimed about one-fifth of each health care dollar for three decades. In contrast, the share of total spending devoted to pharmaceutical products, which is borne largely by individuals, has fallen by half since 1960. Nursing home outlays as a share of health care spending more than doubled between 1960 and 1980 because the proportion of the population over age 80 rose sharply and because medicaid, a program that pays for nursing home care for the aged and disabled poor, was introduced in 1965 (see below).

34. Health Insurance Association of America, *Source Book of Health Insurance Data* (Washington, 1990), p. 31.

35. Health Insurance Association of America, *Providing Employee Health Benefits: How Firms Differ: Results of a 1989 National Survey of Employers* (Washington, 1990), p. 49. For a preliminary evaluation of selected PPOs, see Susan Hosek and others, *The Study of Preferred Provider Organizations: Executive Summary* (Rand Corporation, June 1990).

36. In 1989, 65 percent of such plans required preadmission certification, 54 percent carried out utilization reviews, 44 percent mandated second opinions for surgery, and 39 percent used case management. HIAA, *Providing Employee Health Benefits*, p. 62. For an evaluation, see Congressional Budget Office, *Managed Care and the Medicare Program: Background and Evidence*, CBO Staff Memorandum (May 1990).

37. For example, of those using precertification for hospitalization, second opinions, case management, and utilization review, 35 percent or fewer found them effective. "National Trends in Health Benefits Cost Containment Strategies," *Federation of American Health Systems Review*, vol. 23 (November–December 1990), pp. 38, 39.

Table 3–4. *Outlays and Recipients of Personal Health Care Expenditures, Selected Years, 1960–89*

Year	Total (billions of current dollars)	Recipient (percent)				
		Hospitals	Physicians	Pharma-ceuticals[a]	Nursing homes	Other[b]
1960	23.9	38.9	22.2	17.6	4.2	17.2
1970	64.9	43.0	21.0	13.6	7.6	14.9
1980	218.3	46.9	19.2	9.2	9.2	15.6
1989	530.7	43.9	22.2	8.4	9.0	16.5

Sources: Levit and others, "National Health Care Spending Trends, 1988"; and *HHS News*, December 20, 1990, table 2. Numbers have been rounded.
a. Drugs and other medical nondurables.
b. Dentists' services, other professional services, home health care, vision products, other medical durables, and other personal health care.

Insurance for Acute Care

By 1970 some form of "third-party" payment (payment to the provider by someone other than the patient) accounted for more than 90 percent of hospital revenues (table 3-5). By the 1980s third-party payments approached 95 percent of hospital revenues. In contrast, in 1989 direct payments by patients accounted for about one-fifth of physicians' income, nearly half of nursing home revenues, and about seven-tenths of pharmaceutical revenues.

These statistics document a central fact about modern health care: people directly pay for much of the cost of relatively minor illnesses, but insurance shields most patients against nearly all the costs of hospitalization. Large, infrequent, and unpredictable outlays, such as the costs of hospitalization, are more likely to be insured than are smaller, regular, or more predictable expenses. Households are willing to pay loading charges to avoid large risks, and loading charges are a smaller proportion of large outlays than of small ones. For that reason, hospital benefits were the first to be covered by insurance and remain the best insured.[38]

Insurance for Long-Term Care

Private insurance for long-term care remains a rarity. Only 1.3 million long-term care insurance policies had been sold by 1989, and

38. For a formal discussion of these issues, see Richard Zeckhauser, "Medical Insurance: A Case Study of the Tradeoff Between Risk Spreading and Appropriate Incentives," *Journal of Economic Theory*, vol. 2 (March 1970), pp. 10–26.

Table 3–5. *Source of Payments to Major Health Care Providers, Selected Years, 1960–89*
Percent

Year	Hospitals			Physicians			Pharmaceuticals			Nursing homes		
	Direct payment[a]	Govern-ment[b]	Private insurance[c]	Direct payment[a]	Govern-ment[b]	Private insurance[c]	Direct payment[a]	Govern-ment[b]	Private insurance[c]	Direct payment[a]	Govern-ment[b]	Private insurance[c]
1960	20.4	41.9	36.6	62.3	7.5	30.2	97.6	2.4	0.0	80.0	10.0	10.0
1970	9.0	53.4	37.6	42.6	22.1	35.3	90.9	5.7	3.4	46.9	46.9	4.1
1980	5.2	53.3	41.5	27.0	30.1	43.0	79.6	8.5	12.4	43.5	52.5	4.0
1989	5.5	53.5	41.1	19.0	33.3	47.7	72.4	11.9	15.7	44.5	55.6	2.9

Sources: *HHS News*, December 20, 1990, table 3; and Office of National Cost Estimates, "National Health Expenditures, 1988," *Health Care Financing Review*, vol. 11 (Summer 1990), pp. 26–28. Numbers have been rounded.
a. Patients' out-of-pocket payments.
b. Federal and state and local governments.
c. Private health insurance and other private expenditures.

only 3 percent of these were employer-sponsored.[39] In 1990 only 3 percent of the elderly were covered by long-term-care insurance.[40] In 1989 individuals directly paid 44 percent of nursing home costs, medicaid paid 43 percent, and other sources, including medicare, paid the rest.[41]

Long-term care encompasses both home health services and nursing home care. Use of these services rises sharply with age, and the population over age 85 is projected to more than double over the next three decades. The proportion of the population aged 85 or older living in nursing homes in 1985 was more than eight times as large as the proportion of those aged 65 to 84.[42] The number of people suffering from severe dementia, a problem disproportionately afflicting the very old, is projected to more than double between 1980 and 2020 and to more than double again by 2040.[43] In short, demand for nursing home care and home health services will increase rapidly.

Current methods of paying for long-term care are grossly deficient. Most elderly people cannot afford to pay directly for long-term care for very long without assistance. Among families with a head aged 85 or older, median financial assets were $6,425 in the last half of the 1980s; the annual cost of nursing home care averaged $25,000 in 1988.[44] Only the wealthy or those poor enough to qualify for medicaid can afford nursing home care. Others can gain access to nursing home services only by paying fees they cannot long afford and by depleting assets until they qualify for medicaid.

39. Joshua M. Wiener and Raymond J. Hanley, testimony on the "Federal Employees Long-Term Care Insurance Act of 1989, S.38," presented to the Subcommittee on Federal Services, Post Office and Civil Service, Senate Committee on Governmental Affairs, November 2, 1989.

40. Joshua M. Wiener, "You Can Run, But You Can't Hide: Long-Term Care Financing Reform," testimony presented to the Advisory Commission on Social Security, Washington, December 13, 1990, p. 6.

41. Calculated from data in HHS News, December 20, 1990, table 3.

42. Among the younger group, 19.7 percent had some form of disability; among the latter group, 62.8 percent. Kenneth G. Manton, "Epidemiological, Demographic, and Social Correlates of Disability among the Elderly," Milbank Quarterly, vol. 67, supp. 2, pt. 1 (1989), p. 30. See also Edward L. Schneider and Jack M. Guralnik, "The Aging of America: Impact on Health Care Costs," Journal of the American Medical Association, May 2, 1990, pp. 2335–40. On projections of home care use, see Raymond J. Hanley and Joshua M. Wiener, "Use of Paid Home Care by the Chronically Disabled Elderly," Brookings, June 26, 1990.

43. Robert M. Ball with Thomas N. Bethell, Because We're All in This Together (Washington: Families U.S.A. Foundation, 1989), p. 21.

44. Ball, Because We're All in This Together, p. 13.

Couples of modest means face a cruel choice when one member requires nursing care that cannot be rendered at home. Medicaid rules deny eligibility to couples whose assets exceed modest limits. The paucity of private insurance for long-term care means that the burden of the frail elderly falls on the spouses and children (usually wives and daughters) or other heirs of the elderly, through either reduced inheritances or the obligation to care for the elderly themselves, or on the general taxpayer through taxes to support medicaid.

Similar problems arise with respect to home health care, except that publicly financed home health benefits are negligible in most communities. The range of services that enable people with limitations on activities of daily living to remain in their own homes is broad, and the costs associated with home health care may approximate those of nursing homes. Of 4.6 million chronically disabled elderly people in the United States in 1982, 90 percent received home care from families or friends and 25 percent received some form of paid care. Of the group using paid care, 80 percent also received additional unpaid home care from family and friends. The bulk of empirical research finds no tendency for use of paid home care to supplant unpaid care. Nonetheless, a major concern of those who advocate publicly supported home care or private home care insurance is that the cost of such care will be far higher than estimated because relatives and friends will use the availability of paid care to curtail their own efforts.[45]

The Role of Government

Federal, state, and local governments are involved in providing health insurance in four distinct ways. As employers, governments sponsor insurance for their employees. They manage programs that finance care for the aged and disabled. They also provide health care directly to specific populations. And they influence private insurance through tax and regulatory policies. In addition, the federal government supports a large program of biomedical research, principally through the National Institutes of Health.

45. Raymond J. Hanley and Joshua M. Wiener, "Will Paid Home Care Destroy Informal Support?" Brookings, June 26, 1990. Using two-stage least squares, Hanley and Wiener find that the amount of reported informal care does not decline by a statistically significant amount as formal care increases.

Governments as Employers

Federal, state, and local governments finance health care for their employees. The Federal Employees Health Benefit Plan is the largest single insurance group in the United States. As of March 31, 1990, it covered 2,451,000 federal employees, at least 4 million dependents, and 1.6 million annuitants. The plan is actually an amalgam of 320 separate plans that are sponsored by different federal agencies and are available in relatively comprehensive and restricted forms ("high" and "low" options).[46] State and local governments administer separate plans for most of their 15.3 million employees.

Medicare

Since its implementation in 1966, medicare, the largest government health program, has greatly expanded financial access of the elderly and disabled to acute care. People who have worked in employment covered by social security or railroad retirement are eligible for medicare, which consists of two parts. Part A pays for hospital care and limited nursing home benefits for 33.2 million elderly and disabled beneficiaries and patients suffering from end-stage renal (kidney) disease.[47] Part B covers physicians' charges.[48]

46. The federal employees' health benefit program may have provided a real-life illustration of a theoretical problem with private insurance. Because of the problem of adverse selection, it is possible that no single plan can successfully compete against all possible alternative plans that can be designed. For this reason, no equilibrium set of health insurance plans may exist. See Joseph E. Stiglitz and Michael Rothschild, "Equilibrium in Competitive Insurance Markets: An Essay on the Economics of Imperfect Information," *Quarterly Journal of Economics*, vol. 90 (November 1976), pp. 629–49.

47. Medicare pays the full cost of up to sixty days of hospitalization per illness after the patient has paid a deductible ($628 in 1991) and three-fourths of the cost of the next thirty days per illness. Medicare will also pay half the cost of an additional sixty days of hospitalization that can be used at any time (a lifetime reserve).

48. Part B pays 80 percent of allowed charges for physicians' services over an annual $100 deductible. Physicians may bill patients for the other 20 percent of charges that medicare deems reasonable and for additional amounts if the physicians wish. On 79 percent of claims representing 83 percent of covered charges in 1989, physicians elected to "take assignment," thereby agreeing not to bill patients for any balance. Physicians may decide whether to take assignment on an episode-by-episode and patient-by-patient basis. Assignment rates varied widely by state. *Overview of Entitlement Programs, 1990 Green Book, Background Material and Data on Programs within the Jurisdiction of the Committee on Ways and Means: 1990 Edition*, Committee Print, House Committee on Ways and Means, 101 Cong. 2 sess. (GPO, 1990), pp. 390–400. (Hereafter cited as Committee on Ways and Means, *Background Material*.) Physicians who

The annually adjusted premium, estimated at $358.80 in 1991, covers about one-fourth of program costs.[49] Regular federal budget support supplies the other three-fourths of part B program costs. The heavy subsidy helps explain why almost everyone who is eligible voluntarily buys part B coverage.

A payroll tax pays for part A of medicare. The base for this tax through 1990 was the wage base covered by social security ($51,300 in 1990). Congress set the ceiling on earnings subject to this tax at $125,000 for 1991, to be increased annually by the percentage growth in earnings subject to social security. The proceeds of this tax are deposited in a trust fund from which part A benefits are paid. According to current projections, this tax and accumulated trust fund reserves will cover currently legislated benefits only until 2006.[50] Exhaustion of the trust fund will be delayed if benefits are cut or if economic or demographic trends turn out to be more favorable than those assumed in the projections. Under all plausible projections, however, Congress will have to decide not later than just after the turn of the century whether to curtail benefits, reduce payments to providers, raise payroll taxes, or use general revenues to cover a deficit certain to develop under current law.

Because medicare covers only a portion of personal health care costs of the elderly—85 percent of hospital costs and 64 percent of physicians' services in 1987—most elect to buy supplementary insurance through "medigap" insurance.[51] The best of these plans have well-controlled selling and administrative costs, but some plans pay out less than half of premiums as benefits.

The Medicare Catastrophic Coverage Act passed in 1988 would have extended medicare to cover most of the costs covered by medi-

---

agree to take assignment for all medicare patients in a twelve-month period receive larger payments from medicare, faster reimbursement, and free advertising in directories of participating physicians. Committee on Ways and Means, *Background Material*, p. 137. In the period starting in April 1990, participating physicians accounted for 44.1 percent of those billing medicare. *Medicine and Health*, September 17, 1990, p. 2.

49. The average annual benefit per elderly and disabled person enrolled in 1991 is estimated at $1,915 and $2,115, respectively, under part A and $1,420 and $1,579 under part B. Committee on Ways and Means, *Background Material*, p. 128.

50. 1991 Advisory Council on Social Security, *Report on Medicare Projections by the Health Technical Panel* (March 1991), p. 13.

51. Medicare and medicaid covered only 42 percent of nursing home costs in 1987, but, as noted above, few people buy private health insurance. Waldo and others, "Health Expenditures by Age Group," pp. 111–20.

gap policies, but Congress repealed this act in 1989. It would have waived all cost sharing, other than the deductible, and placed no limit on the number of covered days. It also covered posthospitalization care in skilled nursing facilities and hospice care, with limited cost sharing. The benefits of the Medicare Catastrophic Coverage Act were to be financed by a tax on personal incomes of upper-income elderly persons and by certain other charges. This method of financing led to a sharp shift in political attitudes toward the catastrophic bill for three reasons. First, an energetic campaign of misrepresentation persuaded many whose benefits greatly exceeded their taxes that they stood to lose under the new bill. Second, a minority of high-income elderly correctly perceived that the new act would increase their taxes more than their benefits. Because the current medicare program provides benefits to all of the elderly worth so much more than the medicare payroll taxes they paid, even this group would have remained net beneficiaries from the medicare program taken as a whole. Third, some people objected to taxing only the group that was currently receiving a benefit that everyone could expect one day to receive.[52]

In 1990 Congress imposed important restrictions on medigap policies that required insurers to pay out at least 65 percent of premium income to insured individuals (75 percent to groups), prohibited insurers from denying coverage to elderly persons because of preexisting conditions, and mandated community rating for medigap plans.[53]

Medicaid

Although grouped under a single name, the medicaid program is actually a collection of programs that vary from state to state. Under loose federal guidelines, states pay for acute-care services and for long-term care for low-income households, but eligibility criteria and the mix and generosity of benefits vary enormously. The program has improved access of low-income households to both types of care but is severely flawed in each area.

52. One consequence of the repeal of the Medicare Catastrophic Coverage Act was a sharp rise in the cost of medigap insurance plans bought by most of the elderly. See Milt Freudenheim, "Health Insurers Increase Rates for the Elderly," *New York Times*, April 16, 1990, p. 1.

53. Julie Rovner, "Congress Tightens Regulation of Medigap Insurance Plans," *Congressional Quarterly Weekly Report*, November 3, 1990, p. 3720.

Like medicare, medicaid was enacted in 1965. The federal government offered matching grants to states that agreed to provide certain benefits to specified populations. The federal government also matches payments states elect to make to cover certain additional services and groups. The federal match ranges from 50 percent to 79.8 percent of program costs; states with below-average incomes get the largest matching rates.[54] Mandatory services include inpatient and outpatient hospital benefits; laboratory and X-ray services; skilled nursing facility care for people over age 21; home health care for those eligible for skilled nursing facility care; early periodic screening, diagnosis, and treatment for those under age 21; family planning services and supplies; physician services; and nurse-midwife services. Some states place no limits on these services, while others cap the number of hospital days and physician visits.[55] Many states reimburse providers under medicaid at rates so far below customary charges that many physicians refuse to see medicaid patients.[56] Because fees are so low, any significant increase in the number of people served under medicaid would require raising fees to attract more providers.

Mandatory services and, at state discretion, optional services are available to two classes of recipients. Participating states must provide mandatory benefits to the "categorically needy," including recipients of cash assistance under aid to families with dependent children (AFDC) and supplemental security income (SSI), a cash assistance program serving the poor aged, blind, and disabled.[57]

54. Alicia H. Munnell and Lynn E. Browne with others, "Massachusetts in the 1990s: The Role of State Governments," Federal Reserve Bank of Boston, Research Report 72, November 1990, p. 36.

55. In addition to the mandatory services listed above, states may offer virtually any other health care service (excluding abortions where the life of the mother is not at risk). For example, out of fifty states and three territories, in 1989 fifty-two offered optometric services, twenty-four offered hospice services, and forty-one offered rehabilitative services. Committee on Ways and Means, *Background Material*, pp. 1303, 1304.

56. In 1986 the medicaid fee for a brief follow-up office visit averaged 67 percent of the medicare fee and was less than half in ten states. The medicaid fee for appendectomies averaged 61 percent of that allowed under medicare. As a result, significant minorities of physicians in various specialties refuse to accept medicaid patients. As might be expected, participation varies widely from state to state. *Medicaid Source Book*, Committee Print, pp. 450–52.

57. As of July 1, 1990, states also had to cover pregnant women and young children in families with income and assets low enough to qualify for AFDC and had to provide

States may serve the "medically needy" if they wish.[58] Actual health outlays are subtracted from income in determining whether households qualify. Thus a family with income well above $133\frac{1}{3}$ percent of the maximum AFDC payment may be eligible if medical expenses are sufficiently large.

The cost of a state's program depends on six factors: the range of services and reimbursement; the definition of eligible groups; the number of poor people in the state; the proportion of the eligible population enrolled in medicaid; the rate of use and price of medical services in the state; and, because of the high cost of long-term care, the numbers of elderly and disabled. As a result, medicaid expenditures vary enormously, averaging $219.50 per U.S. resident in 1989, but ranging from $569 per resident in New York to $100 in Nevada.[59] In 1989 the 29 percent of medicaid recipients who were aged, blind, or disabled received $39.4 billion in services, or $5,868 per person. In contrast, AFDC adults and children, accounting for 68 percent of medicaid recipients, received $13.8 billion in services, or $860 per person.[60] The gap between the elderly and nonelderly widened: real per capita benefits for the aged, blind, and disabled had risen about 40 percent since 1975, while the value of medicaid services for AFDC recipients had fallen about 20 percent.

---

limited benefits to all pregnant women and all mandatory benefits to children under age 1 living in families with incomes below federal poverty thresholds. The categorically needy also include people excluded from AFDC for reasons prohibited by medicaid, former AFDC recipients for twelve months after termination of benefits, and, since October 1, 1990, two-parent families where the principal breadwinner is unemployed. Committee on Ways and Means, *Background Material*, pp. 1276–79. The Deficit Reduction Agreement of 1990 added the requirement that by the year 2000 states must provide medicaid coverage for all children in families with incomes at or below federal poverty thresholds. Julie Rovner, "Families Gain Help from Hill on Child Care, Medicaid," *Congressional Quarterly Weekly Report*, November 3, 1990, p. 3721.

58. The medically needy include anyone that the state wishes to cover who is in one of the categories covered by AFDC or SSI and whose income or assets exceed the eligibility limits for cash assistance but whose income is less than $133\frac{1}{3}$ of the maximum AFDC payment for families of the same size. A state may also define as medically needy and thereby extend medicaid to pregnant women and infants with incomes up to 185 percent of the federal poverty threshold and selected other groups.

59. The highest medicaid outlays per person are in the Northeast. Four of the eight lowest-spending states are in the Rocky Mountain area. Oregon, a state that has initiated plans to ration services under medicaid, spends less per capita on medicaid than thirty-nine states and the District of Columbia. Health Care Financing Administration, "Caveats for Basic FY89 HCFA-2082 Data Tables," June 16, 1990, table 9.

60. HCFA, "Caveats for Basic FY89," tables 2, 10.

Governments as Providers

In 1991 total expenditures by federal, state, and local governments on health services to specific groups reached approximately $81 billion. Shown below are these governments' 1991 outlays in billions of dollars.[61]

Program	1991 outlays
Defense Department	15.1
Veterans Administration	12.6
Indian Health Service	1.4
Federal Employees Health	2.4
State and local governments	50.0

These services included health care for members of the military forces and their dependents through the Civilian Health and Medical Program of the Uniformed Services (CHAMPUS);[62] special hospitals and other health services for veterans through the Veterans Administration; and clinic and hospital care for native Americans through the Indian Health Service. State governments maintain psychiatric hospitals. Municipal and county governments support acute-care hospitals serving as providers of last resort, providing care to those who cannot pay for care from other providers or who use these facilities because of convenient location; these facilities received not only public support but also payments under medicare and medicaid and from private insurers.

Taxation

The internal revenue code provides several benefits to encourage health insurance and to support other aspects of the health care industry. No personal income or payroll tax is levied on health insurance financed by employers. The value of this exclusion is

61. *Budget of the United States Government, Fiscal Year 1992*, pp. 4-9, 4-11, 4-636; and author's estimates for state and local governments.

62. CHAMPUS serves active members and dependents of the Army, Navy, Marine Corps, Air Force, Coast Guard, the commissioned Corps of the Public Health Service, and the Commissioned Corps of the National Oceanic and Atmospheric Administration.

projected to rise rapidly. The estimated value for 1991 is $36.3 billion.[63]

In addition, medicare benefits in excess of tax payments represent a form of income for recipients, but unlike most other income they are not taxed. The estimated value of this exclusion was $7.5 billion in 1991.[64] These exclusions, together with the exemption from tax of income from bonds issued by state and local governments for private nonprofit health facilities (estimated 1991 value of $3.2 billion), are equivalent to the combination of direct government expenditures with full and consistent taxation of income. Individuals also may deduct medical costs not reimbursed by others to the extent that these costs exceed 7.5 percent of adjusted gross income (outlay equivalent in 1991 of $3.0 billion).[65]

These tax provisions undergird the system of employer-financed insurance that forms the basis of the U.S. health insurance system. Although not included in the government budget as an expenditure, they contribute to the federal deficit as much as would direct government expenditures of a like amount.

The unlimited exclusion of employer-financed health insurance from personal income tax violates two norms of income taxation: that all income should be taxed and that taxes should influence household consumption choices as little as possible. One purpose of the exclusion of health benefits from personal tax, however, is precisely to distort consumption choices by encouraging employers to help promote private health insurance. The incentive is the difference be-

63. This cost can be calculated in either of two ways: as the difference in revenue between a system that treated the value of health benefits to employees as taxable income and the current system, under which health insurance is excluded from personal income and payroll taxes; or as the added amount employers would have to spend to provide insurance if the benefits, like ordinary compensation, were taxable. The 1991 value of the tax benefits calculated in these two ways is, respectively, $29.6 billion and $36.3 billion. See *Budget of the United States Government, 1992*, table XI-1, p. 3-37.

64. Medicaid benefits are also exempt from tax. But the revenue forgone by this exclusion is trivial because most recipients have incomes so low that few would be subject to personal income tax.

65. The deduction for extraordinary medical outlays, like deductions for casualty losses, rests on the rationale that these expenses are surprise losses equivalent to a destruction of income. In contrast, deduction of routine costs (or exclusion from personal income of the portion of premiums for employer-sponsored insurance that covers routine costs) is not justified under an income tax, because such outlays are seen as routine consumption.

tween the cost to employers of providing workers with health insurance under current rules and the additional taxable wages they would have to pay to enable workers to buy health insurance at the same premiums.[66]

Because they are open-ended, current rules do more than just promote the provision of health insurance. They also encourage relatively generous benefits because the tax concessions are allowed on all employer-sponsored health benefits, however comprehensive the coverage may be. Limiting the exclusion of health insurance premiums from personal taxation to a given dollar amount would preserve incentives for employer-sponsored health insurance but strengthen incentives for cost consciousness at the margin. President Ronald Reagan proposed such a limit in 1982, but Congress did not act on his recommendation. The Treasury Department also included such a limit in the proposals for tax reform issued in 1984, but the White House dropped the limit from its final proposals sent to Congress in 1985, and no limits were enacted in the Tax Reform Act of 1986. The Congressional Budget Office regularly includes such a limit in its list of ways to reduce the federal deficit.[67]

Regulation

Governments regulate the operations of the health care system in countless ways, both important and trivial. States regulate the operations of insurance companies, for example, by mandating the

66. Ordinary income is subject to both payroll taxes and personal income taxes. Health insurance is free of both. The payroll tax rate is 7.65 percent on both employer and employees. Most employees face federal income taxes at marginal rates of either 15 or 28 percent and state personal income taxes at rates that vary from state to state. If the state income tax is assumed to be 5 percent and deductible in computing federal taxes, the cost to employers of paying employees enough to buy $1 of health insurance is 44 percent less than the cost of paying employees in the 28 percent bracket enough to buy $1 of other consumer goods (32 percent less for employees in the 15 percent bracket).

67. In 1990 the CBO estimated that including in taxable personal income the value of employer-financed health insurance above $250 a month for families and $100 a month for individuals would raise over $9 billion a year when fully effective. Denying the exclusion altogether but allowing individuals a credit equal to 20 percent of the value of health insurance up to $250 a month for families and $100 a month for individuals would raise more than $18 billion a year. Congressional Budget Office, *Reducing the Deficit: Spending and Revenue Options, A Report to the Senate and House Committees on the Budget—Part II*, February 1990, pp. 144–46.

inclusion of certain forms of coverage in all insurance plans. They also license providers of all kinds. Along with the federal government, states establish rules and regulations for the medicaid program. The federal government defines certain procedures hospitals and physicians must follow under medicare and regulates the introduction of new drugs.

The federal government has ample power to enforce any regulations it may establish. Apart from the prohibition of criminal activities, the principal governmental tool for compelling compliance by hospitals and physicians is the threat of withholding reimbursement. Since nearly half the revenues of hospitals and more than a quarter of the revenues of physicians in 1989 came from medicare, medicaid, or other federal programs, few providers dare flout federal rules. Congress used this leverage to require hospitals and physicians to secure approval from state agencies for purchases of costly medical equipment. President Jimmy Carter proposed using medicare payments to compel hospitals to comply with cost containment targets, but Congress rejected his proposal.

The federal government can also restrict the policies insurers sell or employers purchase by denying employers the right to deduct the costs of plans that violate federal rules. The Tax Reform Act of 1986 underscored this power by enacting "nondiscrimination" regulations that tightened limits on the proportion of the cost of employer-sponsored fringe benefits that could be paid to high-paid employees. Employers who violated the rules would have lost deductions for these benefits if the law had remained in effect, but Congress repealed it in 1989 because of objections that the requirements were too stringent. However, no one doubted the power of federal instruments to compel compliance. The restrictions on medigap policies enacted in 1990 also display this federal regulatory capacity.

Much of the debate over how best to slow the rapid growth of health care spending centers on the degree to which the federal government, acting alone or in concert with states, should use these regulatory powers to enforce limits on health care spending. Two recent modifications of the medicare program illustrate how rules under this program can influence providers and insurers.

DIAGNOSIS RELATED GROUPS. In 1982 Congress required the Department of Health and Human Services to develop a new system of paying hospitals under medicare. The old system reimbursed hospitals according to the audited cost of services, determined after the patient's discharge. In 1984 the department introduced a reimbursement system in which the payment a hospital receives is set prospectively, based on each patient's primary and secondary diagnoses at time of admission. The Health Care Financing Administration (HCFA) annually sets a schedule of fees for a set of diagnosis related groups (DRGs), currently numbering 477. Hospitals may not bill patients for any amount above the DRG payment.

The objective of the new system is to reduce costs and slow future growth by changing incentives. Under cost-based reimbursement, hospitals had few incentives to economize under medicare because they could count on reimbursement for all reasonable expenditures. Under the DRG system, it is hoped, hospitals try harder to cut costs because they, rather than HCFA, reap the savings. Some evidence suggests that the DRG system has slightly slowed the growth of hospital spending.[68] Furthermore, regardless of the costs hospitals actually incur, the DRG system permits HCFA to directly restrict what it pays by limiting growth of DRG payments and thereby to control the rate at which budget outlays for medicare benefits rise. HCFA has used this power, raising DRG prices by less than the average increase in wages and the price of commodities hospitals buy. After the introduction of the DRG system, a period during which private payers also became increasingly cost-conscious, hospital operating margins on cases subject to DRGs have narrowed sharply, from about 14.5 percent during the first year of the DRG system to roughly zero in the fifth. On all cases, the overall margin of major teaching hospitals turned negative in the fifth year of the prospective payment system. Projections made in 1990 indicated

68. The DRG system controls price, not cost, which is equal to the number of admissions times the cost per admission. Many observers expected admissions to increase after introduction of the DRG system, as hospitals sought to make profits by admitting relatively low-cost patients who previously might have been treated on an outpatient basis; however, admissions actually declined. Since admissions dropped not only for medicare patients but for others, it appears that hospitals were reacting to influences other than the new DRG system. On the issue of the effects of DRGs on costs, see Judith Feder, Jack Hadley, and Stephen Zuckerman, "How Did Medicare's Prospective Payment System Affect Hospitals?" *New England Journal of Medicine*, October 1, 1987, pp. 867–73; and Louise B. Russell and Carrie Lynn Manning, "The Effect of Prospective Payment on Medicare Expenditures," *New England Journal of Medicine*, February 16, 1989, pp. 439–44.

that the trends will continue and that hospitals' negative operating margins will widen, reaching 7 to 14 percent in 1992.[69]

RELATIVE VALUE SCALES. Under Part B of medicare, HCFA has customarily paid physicians 80 percent of "reasonable" charges.[70] This system has resulted in wide variations among fees for physicians that cannot be explained by variations in practice costs among communities or by differences in the length of training among specialties.

In 1989 Congress enacted a fee schedule based on the relative costs of services performed by physicians, but delayed implementation until January 1, 1992. This schedule, named a "resource-based relative value scale" (RBRVS), is based on differences in physicians' time required to render services, practice costs, and malpractice premiums. In addition, Congress required the issuance of volume performance standards for physicians to discourage them from offsetting the effects of any cuts in fees by increasing the number of patient visits.[71]

This RBRVS system is still too new for final judgment. Initial estimates suggest that it will reduce medicare costs by about 12 percent by 1996 when the new payment system is fully effective if physicians' behavior is unaffected, but by only 3.9 percent if physicians change their practice behavior as anticipated.[72] Beyond this initial phase, the RBRVS holds the potential of profoundly changing the cost and composition of physicians' services in several ways. The RBRVS would have its greatest effect if it led to similar changes in payments by other private insurers. It can be used to restrain the growth of medicare spending on physicians' services in ways similar

69. Stuart Guterman, Stuart H. Altman, and Donald A. Young, "Hospitals' Finances in the First Five Years of PPS," *Health Affairs*, vol. 9 (Spring 1990), pp. 125–34; and Thomas Gilligan and Allen Dobson, "Strong Motive for Reform," *Federation of American Health Systems Review*, vol. 23 (September–October 1990), pp. 38–43.

70. Reasonable charges are defined as the smaller of (a) the physician's actual charge, (b) the physician's median charge during a preceding time period for similar services, or (c) the seventy-fifth percentile of the customary charge by physicians for that service in the community.

71. Janet Ochs Wiener, ed., "Physician Payment Reform: Struggling to Be Born," *Medicine and Health*, January 7, 1991. Also see Paul B. Ginsburg, Lauren B. LeRoy, and Glenn T. Hammons, "UpDate: Medicare Physician Payment Reform," *Health Affairs*, vol. 9 (Spring 1990), pp. 178–88.

72. Sandra Christensen and Scott Harrison, *Physician Payment Reform under Medicare*, Congressional Budget Office, April 1990.

to those used in Canada. If used to change the relative incomes of various specialties, the RBRVS may influence the fields of medicine that students choose to enter.[73]

Both the DRG and the RBRVS systems illustrate the power of the federal government to affect the operation of the market for medical services, directly and through the example set for other payers. Furthermore, they indicate the broader power that the government has to transform the character of the medical system.

Research

Since technological change lies at the heart of rising health care expenditures, some observers have suggested reductions in spending on biomedical research to slow growth of health care spending. Expenditures on biomedical research in the United States during 1989 totaled $20.6 billion, slightly more than half under federal sponsorship. The National Institutes of Health (NIH) accounts for just under three-fourths of total federal support. Other sponsoring agencies, in order of size, include the Department of Defense; the Alcohol, Drug Abuse, and Mental Health Administration; the rest of the Department of Health and Human Services (including the Center for Disease Control); the Veterans Administration; the Department of Energy; and the National Science Foundation. Adjusted for inflation, total national support for biomedical research and development rose 65 percent from 1977 through 1989.[74] Despite budget deficits, federal outlays on biological science are projected to rise. The boom in genetic research is driving up privately sponsored research and development as well.

Despite increasing appropriations, applicants for research support from the National Institutes of Health are finding it increasingly difficult to get support. Part of the problem is that in the mid-1980s

73. The RBRVS system may be subject to some of the same problems that afflicted the DRG system. The problem of "DRG creep," the tendency of hospitals to classify newly admitted patients in diagnostic categories that bring increased reimbursement, could easily be repeated under the RBRVS system as physicians shift classification of services rendered to qualify for increased payments. See Gordon R. Trapnell, "The Prospects for Chaos in Fee for Service Based Insurance Plans" (Annandale, Va.: Actuarial Research Corporation, June 1990).

74. Floyd E. Bloom and Mark A. Randolph, eds., *Funding Health Sciences Research: A Strategy to Restore Balance* (Washington: National Academy Press, 1990), p. 32.

NIH managers adopted a policy of committing an increasing fraction of funds projected to be available in the future by lengthening grant periods. The result was a reduction in the proportion of appropriations available for new grants. Another part of the problem is that the number of applications has increased. Thus a declining fraction of applications have won grants, and the scores awarded to winning applications by peer review committees have risen steadily. An additional result has been a sharp reduction in support for training and for investment in laboratories and equipment.

Proposals to reduce research support to slow future growth of health care spending are shortsighted. As noted in chapter 2, new technologies bring large benefits for some patients, but the current financing system also encourages their use in cases where benefits are small. The solution to this problem is not to curtail research, thereby denying help to those patients who stand to receive sizable benefits, but to reform the financing system to curb incentives to provide low-benefit care regardless of cost. In fact, a strong case can be made for increasing the flow of resources both to biomedical research and especially to the training of research scientists and modernization of research facilities.[75]

The Uninsured

In late 1988 31.5 million Americans, or one in eight, lacked health insurance (table 3-6). The proportion of uninsured, which is higher than it was a decade ago, both understates and overstates the seriousness and pervasiveness of problems created by incomplete health insurance coverage. It overstates the problem because many health expenditures are postponable and most of the uninsured will soon be covered. For example, barely one person in twenty-three lacked health insurance continuously from February 1985 through August 1987. However, the number who have no insurance at all on any one date understates the risk of being uninsured; more than one person in four lacked health insurance at some time during this twenty-eight-month period. By this criterion, more than 60 million Americans are at risk of losing insurance. It also ignores those with inade-

75. Bloom and Randolph, *Funding Health Sciences Research*.

Table 3–6. *Characteristics of the Uninsured*
Percent

| | | Period uninsured | |
Characteristic	Fourth quarter 1988	Entire period February 1985– August 1987	At least 1 month in February 1985– August 1987
All persons	13.0	4.3	28.1
Race			
Whites	11.7	4.0	26.4
Blacks	20.2	5.9	37.7
Hispanics	26.5	11.3	52.0
Age			
0–15	15.3	5.1[a]	34.5[a]
16–24	21.9	6.0[b]	51.9[b]
25–44	13.9	4.5	27.7
45–64	9.9	4.3	19.9
64 and over	0.3	0.1	0.7
Region			
Northeast	8.3	1.9	22.1
Midwest	9.2	3.6	24.2
South	17.1	5.9	32.6
West	15.2	5.2	32.1
Income (multiples of poverty threshold)			
Less than 1.0	n.a.	14.8	55.3
1.0 to 1.99	n.a.	8.5	45.7
2.0 to 2.99	n.a.	3.0	29.9
3.0 to 3.99	n.a.	1.7	19.2
4.0 to 5.99	n.a.	0.7	12.8
6.0 and over	n.a.	0.5	8.9

Source: Charles Nelson and Kathleen Short, "Health Insurance Coverage, 1986–88," *Current Population Reports,* series P-70, no. 17 (Department of Commerce, 1990), pp. 4, 5, 9, 17.
n.a. Not available.
a. 0–17 years.
b. 18–24 years.

quate insurance, for example, plans that exclude preexisting conditions—the very problems most likely to require treatment.[76]

Who Are the Uninsured?

A majority of every demographic group, as defined by race and ethnic group, age, place of residence, and income, is insured at any

76. To point up what is at stake, although the uninsured reported that their health status is somewhat worse than that of the insured, they have fewer contacts with physicians and spend fewer days in hospitals. Differences in self-reported health

given moment, but the risk of losing coverage varies widely. Few of the elderly are uninsured, because 98 percent are covered by medicare and most of the rest are covered by other government programs or by private insurance. Young adults are more likely than members of other age groups to change jobs, thereby interrupting coverage under employer-sponsored plans, or to work for employers who do not sponsor plans. For both reasons, they are the age group most often without insurance. More than one-third of all children lacked health insurance at least briefly during the twenty-eight-month period spanning 1985 and 1987.

The likelihood that a person will be uninsured varies by region of residence. In general, residents of the Northeast and the Midwest are about half as likely to be uninsured as are residents of the South and West. These differences largely reflect variations in private health insurance coverage and occur despite broader protection under veterans' or military health plans in the South and West than elsewhere.

Not surprisingly, health insurance coverage rises with income. More than half the people residing in households with incomes below government-defined poverty thresholds lacked health insurance at least briefly between 1985 and 1987. One in seven lacked insurance continuously, a rare circumstance among households with incomes at least twice the official poverty thresholds. Among households with incomes at least six times official poverty thresholds,[77] fewer than one person in eleven was without health insurance even briefly during the period from February 1985 through August 1987.

Trends in the Number of Uninsured

A considerable shadow of uncertainty surrounds estimates of the number of uninsured. It seems clear, however, that the number of uninsured rose in the early 1980s—from an estimated 28.4 million in

---

status may understate actual differences, as contact with physicians may heighten awareness of illnesses.

77. The poverty threshold for a family of four in 1991 is approximately $13,400. Hence this group includes four-person families with annual incomes of at least $80,400 in 1991.

1979 to just under 37 million in the mid-1980s.[78] The sharp decrease in 1988 to 31.5 million cannot be explained by anything that happened in the market for health insurance. Changes in the wording of questions on health insurance in census survey instruments and in the Census Bureau's methods of adjusting responses to remove apparent inconsistencies may explain much of the difference.[79] The increase in the numbers of uninsured from the late 1970s to the mid-1980s seems to have been real, but the decrease by 1988 may be largely an artifact of measurement procedures.

Various forces contributed to the loss of health insurance coverage. Young adults came to account for an increased share of the population. Many employers, smarting under rising insurance costs, shifted premiums to employees, some of whom dropped coverage for dependents or themselves. Other employers simply discontinued plans. In 1981 Congress approved President Reagan's request to narrow eligibility for welfare assistance and thereby excluded many from medicaid coverage. In the late 1980s and 1990, however, Congress extended medicaid coverage to previously ineligible groups.

For reasons stated in chapter 2, the range of private insurance coverage is likely to narrow if current policy remains unchanged. Continually rising premiums will force some employer-sponsors to drop plans and cause others to push up employee cost sharing in an effort to hold down employer premiums. Left to their own devices, insurers will continue to identify high-cost groups, who will then be charged prohibitive premiums or denied coverage altogether. All payers will continue to strive to avoid paying more than the costs they generate, thereby restricting the capacity of hospitals and physicians to provide uncompensated care.[80]

78. *Health Insurance and the Uninsured: Background Data and Analysis*, Committee Print, Subcommittee on Labor-Management Relations and Subcommittee on Labor Standards of House Committee on Education and Labor, Subcommittee on Health and the Environment of House Committee on Energy and Commerce, and Senate Special Committee on Aging, 100 Cong. 2 sess. (GPO, May 1988), p. 110.

79. Katherine Swartz, "Counting Uninsured Americans," *Health Affairs*, vol. 8 (Winter 1989), p. 193; and Swartz, "A Research Note on the Characteristics of Workers without Employer-Group Health Insurance Based on the March 1988 Current Population Survey" (Washington: Urban Institute, January 1990).

80. Stan Jones, "What Is the Future of Private Health Insurance," paper presented to the 3rd Annual Conference and Membership Meeting of the National Academy of Social Insurance, January 24–25, 1991.

Consequences of Lack of Insurance

Common sense suggests that lack of insurance might have some effect on the treatment available to sick patients and hence on the outcomes of treatment. This intuition is remarkably hard to test rigorously, as insured patients differ from uninsured patients in many ways that are relevant to both therapy and health status. Sickly people, for example, are less likely than healthy people to be able to work regularly and hence to qualify for insurance. Whether sickness causes lack of insurance or vice versa is hard to determine precisely.

One study produces disquieting evidence in confirmation of the commonsense intuition.[81] Uninsured patients admitted to hospitals are more likely than insured patients to be admitted on weekends (indicating that the admission is not discretionary and hence that the patients are sicker); they are less likely to receive such discretionary therapies as coronary artery bypass graft surgery and replacement of knees and hips; they are less likely to have normal results on pathological tests (indicating that physicians have higher thresholds for ordering pathological tests for uninsured patients); and they are more likely to die in the hospital. While these results conceivably could be explained by factors other than the availability of insurance, they suggest strongly that the lack of insurance makes a significant difference in therapy and in outcomes of treatment. The idea that the seriously ill receive standard therapy whether or not they have insurance seems to be a comforting delusion.

81. Jack Hadley, Earl P. Steinberg, and Judith Feder, "Comparison of Uninsured and Privately Insured Hospital Patients: Condition on Admission, Resource Use, and Outcome," *Journal of the American Medical Association*, January 16, 1991, pp. 374–79.

CHAPTER FOUR

International Comparisons

INTEREST IN foreign health systems is increasing in the United States. Recent public opinion polls report that U.S. residents are intensely dissatisfied with their health care financing system and think that the system of Canada or some other country is superior.[1] People learn from newspapers and television that infant mortality rates are higher and life expectancy is lower in the United States than in most developed countries and many relatively undeveloped countries despite the fact that U.S. expenditures on health care greatly exceed

1. Two-thirds of surveyed Americans indicated that they would prefer the Canadian health system. Only 10 percent thought that "on the whole, the health care system works pretty well, and only minor changes are necessary to make it work better." Larger proportions of the population expressed agreement with that statement about their own systems in Canada, Netherlands, Germany, France, Australia, Sweden, Japan, United Kingdom, and Italy. See Robert J. Blendon and others, "Satisfaction with Health Systems in Ten Nations," *Health Affairs*, vol. 9 (Summer 1990), p. 188. At the same time, polls indicate that individual Americans are satisfied with their own recent experiences with the health care system. "With regard to their own most recent illnesses, 72 percent of those who were hospitalized in the previous year, 78 percent of those who have seen a physician recently, and 63 percent of those who have needed emergency treatment say that they were completely satisfied with the medical care they actually received." Robert J. Blendon and Drew E. Altman, "Public Attitudes About Health-Care Costs: A Lesson in National Schizophrenia," *New England Journal of Medicine*, August 30, 1984, pp. 613–16. See also Cindy Jajich-Toth and Burns W. Roper, "Americans' Views on Health Care: A Study in Contradictions," *Health Affairs*, vol. 9 (Winter 1990), pp. 149–57.

those of any other nation.[2] Business executives blame the high cost of employer-sponsored insurance for their difficulties in competing with goods made in countries where business directly bears little or none of the cost of financing health care. At the same time, most Americans are unaware of systematic differences between the way the United States reimburses providers of health services and the methods used in most other developed nations.

How much more does the United States spend for health care than other countries? Does it get more health services for its extra outlays? Do international differences in provider reimbursement explain why the United States spends so much? Are such indicators as infant mortality and life expectancy good indices of the quality of the health care system? Would changes in health care financing improve the competitive position of the United States?

Differences in Costs

The health care system of the United States is strikingly more costly than that of any other country in the world (table 4-1). Measured as a fraction of gross domestic product, health care spending in the United States is nearly one-fourth larger than that in the second highest spender, Sweden. Per capita health care outlays are 38 percent higher than those of the second ranking country, Canada. Moreover, these gaps are widening rapidly. Between 1980 and 1987, for example, the share of gross domestic product allocated to health care rose two percentage points in the United States, while it fell in New Zealand, Denmark, Sweden, and Ireland and rose by one percentage point or less in all other European industrial countries and Japan.[3]

2. A typical newspaper story reports that in 1986 the United States ranked twentieth in infant mortality among nations of the world with a rate just twice that of Japan, the leader. See Robert Pear, "Study Says U.S. Needs to Battle Infant Mortality," *New York Times*, August 6, 1990, p. 1.

3. Health care spending as a fraction of gross domestic product grew more rapidly in the United States than in Canada in part because gross domestic product rose faster in Canada than in the United States. However, the excess of per capita spending in the United States over that in Canada, a measure immune to this influence, widened from 29 percent in 1970 to 33 percent in 1980 and 35 percent in 1987. *Health Care Financing Review, 1989 Annual Supplement*, pp. 121, 188, 194.

Table 4–1. *Total Health Expenditures in Selected Countries, 1987*

| | | Per capita outlays[a] | |
| | | | |
Country	Percent of GDP	U.S. dollars	Percent of U.S. outlay
United States	11.2	2,051	100
Sweden	9.2	1,233	60
Canada	8.8	1,483	72
France	8.5	1,105	54
Netherlands	8.5	1,041	51
Austria	8.4	982	48
Germany	8.1	1,093	53
Switzerland	7.7	1,225	60
Norway	7.5	1,149	56
Ireland	7.4	561	27
Finland	7.4	949	46
Belgium	7.2	879	43
Australia	7.2	939	46
Italy	7.2	841	41
New Zealand	6.9	733	36
Japan	6.8	915	45
Portugal	6.4	386	19
United Kingdom	6.0	758	37
Denmark	6.0	792	39

Source: George J. Schieber and Jean-Pierre Poullier, "Overview of International Comparisons of Health Care Expenditures," *Health Care Financing Review, 1989 Annual Supplement,* pp. 2, 4, 121, 190; and author's calculations.
a. Converted at purchasing-power parity rates (based on the income required to buy standard bundles of consumer goods). See appendix A for details.

Age Distribution

These statistics reflect no adjustment for the age composition of the population. Per capita spending on health care rises steeply with age in the United States.[4] It probably does so in other countries as well, although the pattern of increase depends on decisions about the allocation of health care spending among age groups. One can get some sense of the effect of age on health care expenditures if one assumes that the United States had the same age composition as other countries but that relative per capita expenditures by age brackets were unchanged. The proportion of the elderly in 1987 was 10.9 percent in Canada, 12.3 percent in the United States, and 18.3 percent in Sweden. Thus the age-adjusted gap between spending in the United States and spending in countries that have a proportionately

4. Daniel R. Waldo and others, "Health Expenditures by Age Group, 1977 and 1987," *Health Care Financing Review,* vol. 10 (Summer 1989), pp. 116–19.

larger aged population, such as Sweden, is larger than the per capita spending statistics suggest. In contrast, the gap between the United States and countries that have a smaller proportion of elderly persons, such as Canada, is smaller than the spending statistics suggest. The effects can be significant. In 1987 personal health care expenditures in the United States accounted for 9.7 percent of gross domestic product. With the same population profile as Sweden, the United States would have spent an additional 1.4 percent of gross domestic product on personal health care, and with the same age distribution as Canada, it would have spent 0.3 percent less.

Prices

Part of these differences in spending reflect the higher price of medical care in the United States and part represent a greater intensity of services. U.S. physicians earn more relative to average compensation per employee than do physicians of any other OECD country for which data are available.[5] The fee charged for thirteen out of fifteen common medical services was higher in the United States than in the average of up to eight OECD countries, and some of the differences were huge. For example, average fees of U.S. surgeons for appendectomies, cholecystectomies (gall bladder removal), and hysterectomies were about eight times the average for seven European countries and five times the fee in Japan.[6] One study found that although per capita expenditures on physicians' services in the United States exceeded those in Canada by 72 percent, the per capita quantity of physicians' services was actually 28 percent lower in the United States because U.S. fees averaged 139 percent higher.[7]

5. U.S. physicians earned 5.4 times average compensation per worker in 1987, compared with 4.1 in Switzerland (in 1986), 4.3 in Germany (in 1986), 2.5 in Japan (in 1986), 1.8 in Sweden (in 1983), and 3.3 in France (in 1979). *Health Care Financing Review, 1989 Annual Supplement*, pp. 134, 194. Comparisons of absolute compensation are difficult to interpret because amounts hinge on the choice of exchange rates. As an admittedly extreme illustration, Swiss physicians earned 14 percent more than U.S. physicians in 1987 based on official exchange rates but 44 percent less based on purchasing-power parity exchange rates. On this issue, see note 18 and appendix A.

6. Organization for Economic Cooperation and Development, *Financing and Delivering Health Care: A Comparative Analysis of OECD Countries* (Paris, 1987), p. 74.

7. Victor R. Fuchs and James S. Hahn, "How Does Canada Do It? A Comparison of Expenditures for Physicians' Services in the United States and Canada," *New England Journal of Medicine*, September 27, 1990, pp. 884–90.

Composition of Expenditures

The belief that most health care results from scientific determination of the most effective interventions is impossible to reconcile with the gross variations in the composition of health care among countries and the huge differences in the way health services are produced. Are health problems in apparently similar countries really so different that wide variations in rates of hospitalization, lengths of stay, number of visits to physicians, and use of pharmaceuticals are each optimal in particular settings? Are the differences in medical efficacy between diverse approaches to health care quite small? Or are some countries doing a much better job of providing health care than others? And, if so, is it the high users or the low users who are doing the better job? Unfortunately, there are no reliable answers to any of these questions.

TYPES OF CARE. Rates of admission to hospitals and number of bed-days per capita vary widely across nations, as does the frequency with which patients see physicians (table 4-2). Whatever the source of these differences, the use of hospital services in the United States differs markedly from that in other countries. The likelihood that a patient will be hospitalized in the United States is about average among developed nations; but, once admitted, the U.S. patient on the average will be subject to strikingly more intensive treatment and will be sent home much faster than anywhere else (tables 4-2 and 4-3). Hospital expenditures per bed and per patient-day in the United States were far higher than those of any other nation in 1982, and these differences have almost certainly widened since then.[8] The intensity of treatment probably contributes to the relatively short lengths of stay in the United States.

In addition to wide variations in rates of hospitalization, lengths of stay, and numbers of contacts with physicians, the rates at which various invasive procedures are performed differ widely among countries (table 4-4). Of nine common surgical procedures, the U.S. rate was above average for all but two: appendectomies and explora-

8. In 1982 hospital expenditures per bed per year were $122,000 in the United States and $65,000 in Canada. Expenditures per patient-day were $360 in the United States and $210 in Canada. OECD, *Financing and Delivering Health Care*, p. 63.

Table 4–2. *Use of Health Care, Selected Countries, 1987*

Country	Hospital bed-days per person per year	Hospital inpatient admission rates (percent of population per year)	Physician contacts per capita per year
United States	1.7[a]	14.7	5.3[b]
Sweden	4.2	20.0	2.7
Canada	2.0[c]	14.5	6.6
France	3.3[b]	21.2	5.2[b]
Netherlands	3.8	11.0	3.7
Austria	3.3	22.6	5.6
Germany	3.5	21.1	11.5[b]
Switzerland	3.0	13.2	6.0
Norway	4.9	16.3	5.7[c]
Ireland	1.3	16.9	6.5
Finland	4.2	22.6	3.7
Belgium	2.8[b]	14.6[b]	7.4
Australia	3.2[b]	21.6	8.2
Italy	1.6	15.0	10.9
New Zealand	2.1	13.0	3.8[a]
Japan	3.9[b]	7.5	12.8[b]
Portugal	1.1	9.3	2.4
United Kingdom	2.1[b]	15.8	4.5[b]

Source: *Health Care Financing Review, 1989 Annual Supplement*, pp. 140, 141, 143.
a. 1981.
b. 1986.
c. 1985.

tory abdominal surgery (laparotomy), an intervention that has been made unnecessary in many cases by advanced imaging equipment, fiber optics, and other devices. Among the other seven procedures, the U.S. rate was highest for five. The United States also had the highest rate of caesarean deliveries among nineteen countries surveyed in 1981.[9] As shown in table 4-4, not only are rates of surgery in the United States relatively high, but rates also differ greatly among developed nations (as they do among small areas within the United States).

PRODUCTION OF HEALTH SERVICES. Even the staffing of health care systems is highly dissimilar. In 1980 the United States employed 2.8 nurses for each physician, Canada 4.4, Germany 1.4, and Belgium

9. Klim McPherson, "International Differences in Medical Care Practices," *Health Care Financing Review, 1989 Annual Supplement*, p. 15.

Table 4–3. *Mean Length of Hospital Stay for Selected Diseases, Selected Countries*
Days

Country	Lung cancer	Breast cancer	Prostate cancer	Cataracts	Acute myocardial infarction	Pneumonia	Asthma	Stomach or intestinal ulcers	Normal delivery	Hip fracture
United States[a]	8.8	7.1	7.2	1.7	8.9	7.8	4.8	7.1	2.4	14.2
Sweden	n.a.	16.6[a]	13.6[a]	n.a.	10.7[a]	10.8[a]	7.7[b]	n.a.	42.4[a]	15.3[a]
Canada[b]	17.8	14.5	17.0	4.0	14.7	16.8	5.5	10.5	4.2	32.9
France[a]	13.8	7.0	12.7	8.4	12.8	13.4	8.3	13.1	6.3	18.9
Switzerland[a]	16.1	19.3	18.4	11.1	17.8	16.9	14.4	14.1	8.5	33.6
Australia[a]	12.0	11.8	12.4	3.8	10.9	11.6	n.a.	5.1	5.1	25.2
United Kingdom[b]	11.4	12.0	13.0	6.4	11.2	39.9	4.9	10.7	4.3	29.7

Source: *Health Care Financing Review, 1989 Annual Supplement*, pp. 166–71.
n.a. Not available.
a. 1986.
b. 1985.

Table 4–4. *Reported Admission Rates for Nine Common Surgical Procedures, Selected Countries, 1980*[a]
Admissions per 1,000 population

		Admission rates		
Procedure	U.S.	High country	Low country	Average (unweighted)
Tonsillectomy	205	421 (Netherlands)	26 (U.K.)	139
Coronary bypass surgery	61	61 (U.S.)	1 (Japan)	17
Cholecystectomy	203	219 (Canada)	2 (Japan)	101
Exploratory laparotomy	41	116 (U.K.)	41 (U.S.)	88
Inguinal hernia repair	238	238 (U.S.)	67 (Japan)	161
Prostatectomy	308	308 (U.S.)	48 (Sweden)	182
Hysterectomy	557	557 (U.S.)	90 (Japan)	312
Operation on lens	294	294 (U.S.)	22 (Switzerland)	100
Appendectomy	130	340 (Australia)	64 (Norway)	175

Source: Klim McPherson, "International Differences in Medical Care Practices," *Health Care Financing Review, 1989 Annual Supplement*, p. 14.
a. The countries are Australia, Canada, Denmark, Ireland, Japan, the Netherlands, New Zealand, Norway, Sweden, Switzerland, United Kingdom, and United States.

0.3, a pattern that suggests that not all countries are combining the skills of physicians and nurses in an optimal fashion.[10]

The particularly rapid and extensive introduction of new medical technologies in the United States explains a significant part of the difference between the level and growth of outlays in the United States and those elsewhere. Such technologies are far more available in the United States than in the United Kingdom, where per capita spending on health care is approximately one-third of that in the United States (table 4-1).[11] The United States also makes far greater

10. David Parkin, Alistair McGuire, and Brian Yule, "Aggregate Health Care Expenditures and National Income: Is Health Care a Luxury Good?" *Journal of Health Economics*, vol. 6 (June 1987), p. 122. These ratios could be economically optimal if salaries varied more than they actually do.
11. For details on these differences and an explanation of their implications for health care in the two countries, see Henry J. Aaron and William B. Schwartz, *The Painful Prescription: Rationing Hospital Care* (Brookings, 1984).

use of high technology than do Canada and Germany.[12] For example, in 1987 the United States had 7.4 times as many radiation therapy units and 8.0 times as many magnetic resonance imaging units per million people as did Canada and 4.4 times as many open heart surgery units and 2.8 times as many lithotripsy units as did Germany.[13] In addition, the United States provides treatment for end-stage renal disease at a higher rate than any other country.[14]

These comparisons make clear that hospital treatment in the United States is more intense and highly priced, and hence more costly, than elsewhere. Part of the difference in length of stay and intensity of treatment arises because acute-care hospitals in some countries also house elderly patients who might be transferred to nursing homes in the United States.[15] Part of the difference reflects a greater willingness in other countries to allow acute-care patients to convalesce in hospitals rather than at home or in nursing homes. But part of the difference reflects faster release from hospitals, facilitated by intensive use of costly diagnostic and therapeutic procedures. To the extent that faster release from hospitals corresponds to more rapid cures, this last effect is a real saving that should be factored into international comparisons of the cost of medical care.[16] Analysts remain unsure about how much of the international differences are explained by variations in intensity of service or price, or by such other factors as age composition or efficiency in the health care system. Sorting out quality-improving, but cost-increasing, vari-

---

12. Dale A. Rublee, "Medical Technology In Canada, Germany, and the United States," *Health Affairs*, vol. 8 (Fall 1989), pp. 178–81.

13. Bengt Jönsson, "What Can Americans Learn from Europeans?" *Health Care Financing Review, 1989 Annual Supplement*, p. 89.

14. Jönsson, "What Can Americans Learn from Europeans?" p. 88; and *Overview of Entitlement Programs: 1990 Green Book; Background Material and Data on Programs within the Jurisdiction of the Committee on Ways and Means*, Committee Print, House Committee on Ways and Means, 101 Cong. 1 sess. (Government Printing Office, 1990), p. 138.

15. This problem of "blocked beds" has been prominently discussed in the United Kingdom and Canada.

16. Though significant, such adjustments would not change the picture of the U.S. medical system as the most costly in the world. For example, if the additional intensity of treatment reduced the number of bed-days per person by half and this saving in time were reflected in an equal saving in recovery times, the value to the U.S. economy would be approximately $10 billion (valuing each week of recovery time at total private compensation per week). This estimate greatly overstates tangible economic effects, as hospital patients disproportionately consist of the elderly and disabled, whose current earnings are much below average.

ations in technology from simple price changes is a difficult task at best and sometimes impossible because prices for many kinds of health care do not exist in some countries.[17]

Income and Health Care Spending

The United States spends more per capita on health care than other countries do in part because it is richer than other countries.[18] High incomes tend to boost health care spending in two ways: health care is one of the things people buy with higher incomes, and high incomes make health care more costly to produce. This pattern is weakly observable within the United States at any given moment. High-income households spend more on health than do low-income households, but since insurance spares patients most of the costs of health care, the differences are small. Health care spending also rises faster than income within a given country over time, but is even more sensitively related to income across countries at a given point in time. This relationship arises in part because high incomes consist largely of high wages and salaries. Salaries of health care personnel must be high enough to attract workers from other occupations in which international differences in productivity are likely to be far more pronounced than in health care delivery. In the extreme case, if health care workers' productivity were similar in all nations but their compensation varied in proportion to average per capita income, and if the cost of health care consisted entirely of such wages and salaries, then per capita spending on health care would be proportional to per capita national income, but real per capita consumption of health care services would not vary with income.[19]

17. See appendix A.

18. If currency units of various nations are converted into dollars at rates based on the income required to buy standard bundles of consumer goods ("purchasing-power parity" exchange rates), the United States remains the richest industrial nation in the world. Based on conventional exchange rates used in international trade and capital transactions, per capita income in the United States is lower than that in several other countries. Conventional exchange rates are based only on internationally traded goods and services and capital movements. Purchasing-power parity rates also take account of goods and services that are not traded, such as housing and wholesale and retail trade; the United States appears to be more efficient than other countries in these activities.

19. That is, the income elasticity of demand for health care across nations would be 1.0. In this situation, the mystery would be what factors caused the income elasticity of demand for health care to differ from 1.0.

In fact, of course, productivity of health care workers is probably higher in high-income countries than in low-income countries, as the educational and other advantages that contribute to the productivity of workers in one sector are likely to be at work in others. Furthermore, the availability of more and better health care facilities in high-income countries will enhance productivity of health care workers. To this extent, higher payments to health care workers are not associated with higher prices, but reflect a larger quantity of health care services. Furthermore, differences in the prices of medical equipment and pharmaceutical products are limited by international trade.[20]

In short, international comparisons of per capita health care spending are not a good guide to the per capita consumption of health care services. One would expect per capita expenditures on health care to be higher in high-income countries than in low-income countries even if there were no difference in the actual per capita consumption of health care, but actual differences in spending are larger than such price differences could explain.[21]

Actual health care spending in the United States is nearly one-fourth higher than is suggested by estimates of a simple relationship

20. For example, the cost of modern imaging equipment, which is manufactured by a few companies and is traded internationally, is similar everywhere. Particular kinds of machinery, such as X-ray equipment or CT scanners, come in various models with varying numbers of "extras." X-rays can be delivered with different degrees of accuracy and power by machines of different design at widely varying cost. Furthermore, there is an active market in used machines of older designs. The question in all of these cases is how to treat the fact that used machines or ones of older design do not do quite as good a job as newer machines of more advanced design. This question is baffling because good data are lacking on the effect of such differences in technical performance on patient outcomes, and no one has attempted to put an explicit value on any such variations. Hence it is currently impossible to determine how much of the added cost of the "best" equipment shows up as "more" health care and how much is just higher price.

21. Since personnel costs represent about 58 percent of the cost of hospital care and an even larger share of ambulatory care, a difference in health care spending of at most 5 to 7 percent for each 10 percent difference in income (an income elasticity of 0.5 to 0.7) would signify little *real* international difference in per capita consumption of health care, if the remuneration of health care personnel relative to average national income and productivity per worker were similar across nations. However, the data indicate that per capita health expenditures differ not by 5 to 7 percent, but by roughly 13 percent for each 10 percent difference in per capita gross domestic product. Jönsson, "What Can Americans Learn from Europeans?" p. 83. Using data from 1980 and a

between income and health care outlays.[22] Four possible explanations for such high spending may explain this gap. First, health care providers may be remunerated even more generously in the United States than its high per capita income would suggest. Second, the United States may be spending relatively more than other countries on health services of little of no medical benefit (see chapter 2). Third, U.S. methods of producing health care may be less efficient than other countries', in the sense that care of equal or nearly equal benefit could be provided at reduced cost. Finally, the United States may be buying an even larger quantity of beneficial health care relative to its income than other countries.

At present no one really knows the relative importance of these four possible explanations, in large measure because solid information on the efficacy of various interventions is so sparse. Even if the efficacy were clear, however, the question would remain of whether the medical benefits flowing from greater U.S. outlays were worth the added costs incurred in providing them.

Measures of Health Status

Although the United States spends more on health care than any other country, among OECD countries the United States is about average in life expectancy (see table 4-5) and much above average in infant mortality rates.[23] The coincidence of high spending on health

---

variety of functional forms to estimate the relationship, Parkin, McGuire, and Yule found elasticities of per capita health expenditures to per capita gross domestic product ranged from 0.8 to 1.6 if currency units were converted with conventional exchange rates and from 0.8 to 1.1 if purchasing-power parity exchange rates were used. See "Aggregate Health Care Expenditures and National Income," p. 118.

22. A statistical relationship between income and health care spending estimated by Jönsson indicates that U.S. per capita outlays in 1986 would have been $1,472, 28 percent below actual outlays of $1,886. Jönsson, "What Can Americans Learn from Europeans?" p. 82.

23. Between 1960 and 1980, the United States slipped from eleventh to twentieth place among twenty-four OECD countries in infant mortality. As shown in table 4-5, life expectancy in the United States is about average among OECD countries, except at age 80, when life expectancy in the United States is relatively high. The relatively high life expectancy at age 80 could have at least three explanations with radically different implications for policy. First, this age group may consist of people who reached maturity during a period when nutrition was better and physical hazards

Table 4–5. *Life Expectancy in the United States and U.S. Rank among Selected Countries, by Age and Sex*[a]
Years

Country and sex	Age			
	Birth	*40*	*60*	*80*
United States				
Females	78.3	40.3	22.5	8.8
	(13/24)	(11/23)	(11/23)	(2/20)
Males	71.5	34.7	18.2	6.9
	(16/24)	(11/23)	(11/23)	(3/20)
Leading country				
Females	81.4	42.5	24.0	8.9
Males	75.6	37.4	19.9	7.5

Source: *Health Care Financing Review, 1989 Annual Supplement*, pp. 177–84. Comparison based on data for various years.

a. Numbers in parentheses are U.S. rank out of number of countries shown.

care in the United States and mediocre health outcomes has led some observers to conclude that U.S. health care spending is misdirected. While the conclusion may be correct, statistics about infant mortality and life expectancy are not conclusive evidence for at least three reasons.

First, these are crude indicators of health status. The major part of modern health care serves not to reduce mortality but to speed cures, reduce disabling side effects of illnesses, or provide succor to the sick. The United States, for example, spends more than $15 billion a year on coronary artery bypass surgery and coronary angioplasty, procedures to improve circulation to the heart when coronary arteries become partly blocked.[24] Repeated studies have shown that these

were lower in the United States than in most other countries. Second, alone among age groups in the United States, the elderly enjoy almost universal financial access to health care because of medicare. Third, those who survive to very old ages are genetically strong or environmentally privileged. The first explanation would highlight the importance of public health measures broadly defined to include public safety, environmental improvement, and measures to promote healthful diets, as well as the importance of narrowing overall income inequality. The second explanation would suggest making standard health care more widely available to those who now cannot afford it or promoting use of available services. The third explanation would mean that the high life expectancy of the elderly carried no policy implications whatsoever. Unfortunately, no good evidence is available on whether one or more of these explanations is valid.

24. In 1988 coronary artery bypass surgery was performed on 353,000 patients, angioplasty on 227,000. Edmund J. Graves, *1988 Summary: National Hospital Discharge Survey*, Advance Data no. 185, National Center for Health Statistics, June 19, 1990.

procedures extend life expectancy in only a minority of cases. Usually, the procedures reduce pain or increase capacity for work and exercise. Some part of this surgery, no doubt, is medically unnecessary. If life extension were the only objective, the United States could save billions. The benefits of this procedure will not show up in statistics on life expectancy or infant mortality. Whether or not the expenditures for coronary bypass surgery and angioplasty are good uses of national resources, most go toward the medically legitimate objective of improving the quality of life, not extending it.

Second, while health care services influence the health of a nation, so do public health measures, income, crime and other forms of violence, consumption and eating patterns, environmental hazards, and, perhaps, genetic differences. For example, age-specific death rates from coronary disease among 45- to 64-year-olds fell about 3 percent a year between 1970 and 1985 for white men and nonwhite women for reasons that remain unclear but may include increases in exercise and reductions in smoking and consumption of red meat, eggs, and butter. In contrast, the likelihood that a person aged between 15 and 24 would be murdered almost tripled between 1960 and 1988.[25]

Third, even if health services were optimally distributed, health care spending might be either negatively or positively related to measures of public health. If nations face similar health environments, but some spend more than others on health services, the relationship between health care spending and measures of health outcomes would be positive. In contrast, if various nations adopted similar health care policies but some enjoyed more salutary health environments than others and hence placed relatively few demands on their health care systems, health care spending would be negatively related to health outcomes.

Some evidence suggests that the problems facing personal health care services in the United States are indeed more formidable than those confronting health care in other nations. Health status is positively correlated with income. A larger fraction of the U.S. popula-

25. *Overview of Entitlement Programs: 1990 Green Book*, Committee Print, p. 909; and National Center for Health Statistics, "Monthly Vital Statistics Report," vol. 39 (November 1990), p. 21, table 7. For more general arguments regarding the dominance of factors other than health care as determinants of health status, see Victor R. Fuchs, *Who Shall Live?* (Basic Books, 1974); and *A New Perspective on Health of Canadians: A Working Document* (Ottawa: Information Canada, 1975).

tion, especially of children, is poor than is the case in other developed nations.[26] Thus the U.S. ranking on life expectancy and infant mortality could be mediocre because of serious problems afflicting a few groups and despite efficient allocation of health care among the mass of the population. Indeed, persuasive evidence suggests that the overall well-being of the American population could be improved in important ways if health services were redistributed or increased for those who are underserved.[27]

The central point is that the rather laggard infant mortality rates and average life expectancies of the United States, although unfortunate, do not by themselves imply anything about the allocation of health care resources. These facts could as easily mean that people's behavior in modern societies—toward others and toward themselves—has a larger bearing on health outcomes than does the health care system. The case that health care resources are misallocated in the United States must, and can, be sustained with other evidence.

Differences in Organization

The diverse institutional arrangements adopted in industrial countries to help people pay for health care conceal a deep structural similarity. People may be covered by insurance companies, special savings accounts (sickness funds), or the government. To pay for this coverage, the government may impose taxes; employers may make voluntary or mandatory payments; or individuals may buy insurance coverage. Arrangements for reimbursing hospitals, physicians, and other health care providers vary widely. But in all cases, societies spare most patients most of the cost of medical care at the time of illness. Contemplating this underlying similarity, one analyst wrote:

> We spend too much time arguing about the relative merits of consumers giving money to private insurance companies in the form of premiums as opposed to giving the money to government

26. Timothy M. Smeeding and Barbara Torrey, "Poor Children in Rich Countries," *Science*, November 11, 1988, pp. 873–77.

27. Jack Hadley, Earl P. Steinberg, and Judith Feder, "Comparison of Uninsured and Privately Insured Patients: Condition on Admission, Resource Use, and Outcome," *Journal of the American Medical Association*, January 16, 1991, pp. 374–79.

Table 4–6. *Public Expenditures as a Share of Health Care Spending,*
Selected Countries, 1987
Percent

Country	Total health expenditures	Hospitals	Ambulatory care
Australia	70	80	61
Austria	67	42	59
Belgium	77	53	86
Canada	74	88	71
Denmark	86	100[a]	69[a]
Finland	79	91	75
France	75	90	63
Germany	78	85	73
Greece	75	45[a]	25[b]
Iceland	89	n.a.	n.a.
Ireland	87	n.a.	n.a.
Italy	79	89	77
Japan	73	93	85[a]
Luxemburg	92	96	86
Netherlands	74	83	63
New Zealand	82	97[a]	96[a]
Norway	98	100[a]	n.a.
Portugal	61	n.a.	75[c]
Spain	71	77[c]	n.a.
Sweden	91	n.a.	n.a.
Switzerland	68[a]	82[a]	n.a.
United Kingdom	86	n.a.	n.a.
United States	41	52	24

Source: *Health Care Financing Review, 1989 Annual Supplement*, pp. 121–26.
n.a. Not available.
a. 1986.
b. 1982.
c. 1984.

(local or national) in the form of taxes. This is not the critical distinction. The most important factor is what the recipient of the money, or the third-party payer (public or private), does with it and what pressure that third-party payer brings to bear on the provider community.[28]

In one respect, however, foreign systems closely resemble one another and differ from that of the United States. Public expenditure plays a far larger part in health care systems abroad than in the United States (table 4-6). The difference is particularly striking in

28. Jack A. Meyer, Comments on Bengt Jönsson, "What Can Americans Learn from Europeans?" *Health Care Financing Review, 1989 Annual Supplement*, p. 109.

the case of hospitals, the largest component of health care outlays. Governments directly supply 90 percent or more of the entire hospital budget in seven OECD countries. In the United States, by contrast, numerous payers, private and public, underwrite hospital spending.

The major arrangements for reimbursement of hospitals and physicians in selected OECD countries are shown in table 4-7. All countries included there, other than Japan and the United States, pay hospitals according to prospectively established budgets or per diem rates for ordinary operating costs and pay for capital investments with separate budgets. Reimbursement of physicians is highly varied, with different arrangements for general practitioners or specialists and for services rendered in or out of hospitals.

Public control of hospital budgets creates an opportunity to control health care spending through use of annual budgets. Whether the prevalence of such control in other countries contributes to their lower total expenditures on health care is a matter of some dispute. Similar controls existed during the 1960s and 1970s, when several other countries spent nearly as large a part of their national incomes on health care as did the United States. The gap between spending in the United States and abroad has opened since the mid-1970s, when economic growth in all developed countries slowed. Although hard evidence is lacking, it appears that central budgetary controls over the hospital sector gave other countries the capacity to clamp down on health care spending when the economic climate deteriorated.[29]

International Competition

The combination of employer-sponsored and -financed health insurance with relatively faster growth of costs has led many U.S. employers to blame health care costs for their difficulty in competing

29. Whether a large public-sector presence results in reduced health care spending has been a matter of some academic dispute. One study based on data from 1974 found that the share of public spending in health outlays was *positively* associated with per capita national health care expenditures. Robert E. Leu, "The Public-Private Mix and International Health Care Costs," in Anthony J. Culyer and Bengt Jönsson, eds., *Public and Private Health Services: Complementarities and Conflicts* (Oxford: Basil Blackwell, 1986), pp. 41–63. The estimated positive effect of public spending was sizable—an increase in the public share from 41 percent (the U.S. share) to 100 percent would increase per capita health care spending by an estimated 35 percent. The same

with foreign companies that directly bear little or none of these costs. Spokespersons for the automobile industry, for example, claim that each U.S. automobile incorporates $500 to $700 of health care costs, while foreign producers of cars do not have to bear such costs.[30]

The argument that high health costs undermine competitiveness contains four links: (1) health care costs raise labor costs; (2) higher labor costs boost cost of production of affected companies; (3) higher production costs raise dollar prices; (4) higher dollar prices damage the capacity of U.S.-based producers to meet competition in the United States or abroad. While this argument seems appealing, even indubitable, the first and fourth links are basically incorrect. In general, relatively high average health care costs in the United States have little or no effect on *overall* U.S. competitiveness. Companies with health care costs higher than the U.S. average—those with large obligations to retirees or particularly generous plans for active workers—may suffer some competitive disadvantage; paradoxically, companies with lower than average costs may enjoy a competitive advantage.

Compensating Differences in Wages

The first link of the preceding argument is weak because companies are primarily interested in the total cost of compensation for workers—cash wages and all fringes taken together—not just in the cost of a single component of compensation. Although businesses seek to provide the combination of wages and fringe benefits of greatest appeal to workers, most companies care less about how compensation is distributed between wages and fringes than they do about the total cost. Companies with rising health insurance bills are able to afford smaller increases in cash wages or other fringe benefits than they could if health insurance costs were stable or falling. Thus the argument that high health costs hinder competition ignores the pressure on employers to try to offset high health costs by restricting other elements of compensation. If other employment costs are suppressed enough to offset the higher health costs, total

equation that produced this result, reestimated on data for 1986–88, indicates that public expenditure has a *negative* effect on overall spending. See appendix B.

30. See Uwe E. Reinhardt, "Health Care Spending and American Competitiveness," *Health Affairs*, vol. 8 (Winter 1989), pp. 5–21.

Table 4-7. *Reimbursement and Planning Arrangements in Selected OECD Countries*

Arrangement	Canada	United Kingdom	France	Sweden	Germany	Japan	United States
Reimbursement							
Hospitals							
Operating costs	Annual prospective budgets controlled by provincial governments	Annual prospective global budget set by Parliament	Annual prospective global budget	Annual budgets, set by local community councils	Prospective, hospital-specific per diems negotiated with hospital and regional associations	Fee-for-service	Diagnosis related fees for medicare; predominantly retrospectively based fees
Capital costs	Separate capital budgets; specific approval of projects by provincial governments	Separate capital budgets controlled by central government	Amortization through charges and capital grants from government	Community-financed by specific appropriations voted by community councils	Lump-sum grants for short-lived equipment; specific grants for structures or long-lived equipment	Fee-for-service payments; public loans for private hospitals, government grants for public hospitals	Fee-for-service or charity, except for medicare, which includes separate capital grants
Physicians							
Ambulatory sector							
General practitioners	Fee-for-service (salaries in health centers)	Capitation (fee-for-service for selected procedures)	Fee-for-service	n.a.	Fee-for-service	Fee-for-service	Fee-for-service (salary and complex contracts in HMOs and PPOs)

Specialists	Same	Salary (fee-for-service for home visits)	Same	n.a.	Same	Same	Same

Hospital sector							
General practitioners	Fee-for-service if self-employed; salary if physician-employed	Salary	Salary, public hospitals; fee-for-service, private hospitals	n.a.	Salary, when in training	Fee-for-service	Fee-for-service and salary (salary and complex contracts in HMOs and PPOs)
Specialists	Same	Same	Same	n.a.	Salary, except fee-for-service for private patients of chiefs of departments	Same	Same
Health-sector planning	Planning capacity of health system fully determined by provincial governments	Carried out by regional and district authorities that control all health care capacity other than a few private hospitals	Regional and national planning; national health plan determines capacity of the hospital system	Capacity determined at local level; no formal national health planning	Capital investments subject to statewide planning, which determines capacity of system	Public hospitals (40 percent of total) subject to prefectural permits for expansion	Limited planning through requirements of state-authorized "certificate of need" for major investments

Sources: Uwe E. Reinhardt, "The Compensation of Physicians: Approaches Used in Foreign Countries," *QRB* (December 1985), pp. 366–77; and Organization for Economic Cooperation and Development, *Financing and Delivering Health Care: A Comparative Analysis of OECD Countries* (Paris, 1987), pp. 27, 28.

n.a. Not available.

production cost is unaffected. The company's capacity to compete, inside the United States or abroad, is unchanged.

Of course, not all companies with higher than average health care costs are able to suppress cash wages or other fringe benefits. Indeed, some of the industries with the most liberal health care benefits also pay higher than average wages. The automobile industry is the prime example. Both high wages and generous health care benefits reflect the considerable market power automobile unions enjoyed for many years. High growth of health insurance costs will force such companies to raise prices enough to maintain a sufficient profit margin. The high prices that result from total costs of compensation (not just from high health insurance costs) will reduce the capacity of such companies to compete not just with imports but with other domestic companies. Some companies can fully offset high health insurance costs by reductions in other wage costs, while some cannot. Overall, the amount by which high health insurance costs push up average prices will depend on the size of these two groups.

Average Health Costs and Dollar Prices

High average health care costs would not affect U.S. competitiveness if all prices rose proportionately. This surprising conclusion follows from the identity relating national product to national income that determines the relation between U.S. exports and U.S. imports, or the balance of trade.

U.S. national product (NP) consists of four major components: consumer goods (C), investment goods used domestically (I), government services (G), and the difference between U.S. exports (X) and imports (M). National income (NI) may be used for three purposes: to buy consumer goods (C), to pay taxes (T), or to increase assets through private saving (S). In symbols, since NP is equal to NI by definition, $C + I + G + (X - M) = C + T + S$. Subtracting C from both sides and rearranging terms, $(I - S) + (G - T) = (M - X)$. The quantity, $I - S$, is the excess of domestic investment over private saving; $G - T$ is the government deficit; and $M - X$ is the international current account deficit.

Overall U.S. competitiveness in international markets is measured by the current account balance, which exactly equals the excess of domestic investment over private saving, plus the government deficit. This relationship holds whether national income and product are large or small. It means that a change in health insurance costs, or any other production cost, can affect the *overall* U.S. trade position only if it changes the difference between domestic investment and saving or if it changes the government deficit.[31]

There is no obvious reason why an increase in health care costs should change the balance between private saving and domestic investment, and if there were an effect it could go either way. High health costs do imply increased costs for government-sponsored health insurance, which could somewhat boost the budget deficit if not offset by cuts in other spending or by additional taxes. Most state and local governments operate under balanced budget requirements. Added federal health care spending under medicare should not materially affect fiscal policy goals, which are expressed in terms of the overall deficit.

What this means is that any increase in the average price of U.S. goods and services attributable to health care costs will be offset by automatic adjustments in the exchange value of the U.S. dollar sufficient to offset these price effects.[32] If U.S. dollar prices are, say, 2 percent higher than they would otherwise be because of health costs, a shift in the exchange value of the U.S. dollar by 2 percent would leave the international competitive position of U.S. goods at home and abroad unchanged.

Cross-Company Variations in Health Care Costs

High health care costs do not affect all producers equally, however. Specifically, labor compensation is a larger part of total produc-

31. The text equations refer to total expenditures. At given prices, changes in total expenditures are proportional to changes in quantities. But changes in quantities demanded or supplied normally require some change in price. Thus a rise in the budget deficit will tend to reduce U.S. competitiveness expressed as an increase in the trade deficit (or a decrease in the trade surplus). For this outcome to occur, the exchange value of the U.S. dollar would have to rise, raising the price of U.S. products for foreign purchasers and lowering the price of foreign products for U.S. purchasers. As a result, U.S. companies would sell smaller quantities abroad and foreign companies would sell more in the United States. That is exactly what a loss of international competitiveness means.

32. The relevant average price is that for goods and services that are involved in international trade, in the sense that they are exported or are in competition with imports.

tion costs for some companies than for others. Some companies offer much larger health benefits to active workers and to retirees than do others. Among retirees with employer-sponsored postretirement health benefits in 1988, more than 90 percent had been employed in firms with 1,000 workers or more and more than 70 percent in manufacturing.[33] Companies that have larger than average health care obligations to active and retired workers and do not or cannot reduce cash wages or other compensation sufficiently can meet their obligations only by boosting the prices they must charge to make a given profit. These companies will tend to lose markets in the United States and abroad to domestic and foreign competition.

But the converse holds for companies that have relatively low labor costs per dollar of value added or that offer low health benefits or none at all. The high average cost of U.S. health care will affect their prices less than the average for all U.S. companies. And the adjustment in exchange rates, which is based on the average price effect from health costs, will more than compensate such companies for the less than average burden of health care costs. The competitive position of these companies will actually be strengthened.

In summary, high and rapidly growing U.S. health care costs do not much affect *overall* U.S. international competitiveness, but they may influence the composition of U.S. exports and imports. For example, high costs of labor compensation, consisting of both high wages and costly health insurance benefits for active workers and large obligations to retirees, no doubt add to the difficulties American automobile companies face in competing with foreign-owned companies. To an increasing extent, auto sales are lost to relatively new, domestically located, foreign-owned companies, not just to imports, because those companies do not have a large pool of retirees who claim health benefits.[34] But to the extent that such companies' large

33. Michael A. Morrisey, Gail A. Jensen, and Stephen E. Henderlite, "Employer-Sponsored Insurance for Retired Americans," *Health Affairs*, vol. 9 (Spring 1990), pp. 57–73.

34. Pension obligations to retirees and to older active workers create similar problems to the extent that companies have not already set aside reserves adequate to pay for those obligations and to the extent that the work forces of U.S.-owned domestic enterprises are older than the work forces of foreign-owned enterprises located in the United States. Age is relevant because pension plans established before the enactment of the Employee Retirement Income Security Act in 1974 may not have accumulated

obligations for health care costs worsen the U.S. balance of trade, the associated reduction in the exchange value of the U.S. dollar opens market opportunities for other U.S. companies.

Much more important than the effects on international trade of U.S. health care policies is whether resources devoted to health care are used wisely. It matters a great deal for the welfare of American consumers whether expenditures on an industry that accounts for one-eighth of total national output are well spent and whether the industry is well organized to produce high-quality services at least cost. Poor decisions directly lower consumer welfare.[35] But U.S. competitiveness as measured by its trade balance will be determined by whether U.S. saving, private and public, is sufficient to support U.S. investment, not by whether particular corporations and unions years ago negotiated obligations that now hobble those companies.

Implications of Foreign Experience

The U.S. health care system compares poorly by broad indicators with European and Canadian systems, but performs well in many specific areas. While European and Canadian systems provide universal financial access to health care, they also restrict spending sufficiently to force curtailments of amenities or rationing of certain services, especially those dependent on high technology; as a result, a modest proportion of their relatively wealthy citizens opt to buy health care from private providers outside the national health care system.[36] In addition, the instruments by which other countries have

---

enough reserves to pay off accrued liabilities. As a result, the costs to fund these benefits must come out of current production.

35. As Uwe E. Reinhardt observed: "Even if every increase in the cost of employer-paid health care benefits could immediately be financed by the firm with commensurate reductions in the cash compensation of its employees—so that 'competitiveness' in the firm's product market is not impaired—it would leave employees worse off unless the added health spending bestowed upon employees is valued at least as highly as the cash wages they would forgo to finance these benefits. . . . Therein . . . lies the most powerful rationale for vigorous health care cost containment on the part of the American business community." Reinhardt, "Health Care Spending and American Competitiveness," p. 20.

36. Uwe E. Reinhardt, Comments on Bengt Jönsson, "What Can Americans Learn from Europeans?" *Health Care Financing Review*, 1989 Annual Supplement, pp. 102–03.

achieved universal access to health care and superior control over growth of spending have spawned problems of their own. Critics complain of a shortage of equipment necessary to implement technological innovations.[37] Patients see themselves as powerless before government-managed bureaucracies.[38] Few pressures exist to design innovative ways of delivering health care or of promoting efficient resource use, such as prepaid group practice, health demonstrations, and social experiments.[39]

In contrast, the U.S. health care system provides high-quality care to most of the 85 percent of the population that is insured and to those among the uninsured with sufficient income. But a sizable minority of the U.S. population depends on uncompensated services of physicians and hospitals and suffers some restriction on the use of services. Furthermore, the failure of U.S. efforts to control growth of spending has been consistent and spectacular.

In reforming its health care system, the United States faces two broad classes of problems. The first is how to achieve the universality of access to health care that is commonplace in other countries. Some have done so through direct government control of health care financing. Others have required people to belong to one or another private-sector group plan, while providing backup public coverage. In general, however, other countries have made health care an entitlement guaranteed by law to almost all residents.

The second problem is how to reduce the quantity of relatively low-benefit, high-cost care. Other countries have unquestionably kept per capita health care spending well below that in the United States. They have used global budgets—typically enforced through many separate regions, not uniformly over the nation—to control hospital costs.[40] The United States, in contrast, has adhered to a

37. See, for example, Edward Neuschler, *Canadian Health Care: The Implications of Public Health Insurance* (Washington: Health Insurance Association of America, June 1990).

38. Björn Lindgren, Comments on Alain C. Enthoven, "What Can Europeans Learn from Americans?" *Health Care Financing Review, 1989 Annual Supplement*, p. 68.

39. Alain C. Enthoven, "What Can Europeans Learn from Americans?" *Health Care Financing Review, 1989 Annual Supplement*, pp. 49–63; and Aaron and Schwartz, *Painful Prescription*.

40. "The European systems have been able to reduce the total costs of health care not so much through central planning and regulation as through global budgets at the regional level. In fact, the role of the central government in health care policy has never been as strong in Europe as is perhaps thought in the United States, and during

highly decentralized system of insurance and of payment to providers. For reasons presented in the next chapter, the United States is not going to be able to make significant progress in simultaneously extending access to health care and controlling growth of spending unless it adopts laws that require coverage and coordinates payments to hospitals and physicians to achieve cost control.

Appendix A: Intertemporal and International Comparisons of Health Care Expenditures

Comparison of real expenditures on any commodity over time and across space requires the separation of changes in total expenditures into changes in price and changes in quantities produced or sold. Expenditures on any commodity can be interpreted as a measure either of the quantity of the good that is produced or bought or of the quantity of other goods that must be sacrificed or forgone to make the particular good available. At any moment this distinction is without significance. When one compares expenditures over time or space, however, a problem arises, because the price of one commodity relative to the price of other goods may not be the same at different dates or places. In addition, particular problems associated with the measurement of the price of health care and of the quantity of health care services distort such comparisons to the point of meaninglessness.

Intertemporal or international comparisons of health care expenditures suffer from a particularly virulent form of these problems. First, the price of health care services as officially measured has risen faster than that of other commodities. As a result, a larger quantity of other goods must be forgone now than in the past simply to provide the same quantity of health care. Some of this increase in price is probably just that—a rise in the price of goods and services hospitals provide relative to the price of other products. But some of the reported increase in price is probably improvement in the quality of care that

---

the 1980s there has been a strong trend toward decentralization. Compared with Europe, the U.S. Federal Government seems to have less control over the totality of the system, at the same time that it is more directly involved in detailed regulation of efficacy, safety, and price setting." Jönsson, "What Can Americans Learn from Europeans?" p. 92.

has been mislabeled as an increase in price. For example, the number of hospital employees per patient has risen dramatically—from 272 per 100 patients in 1971 to 392 per 100 patients in 1986; much of this increase reflects the expanded menu of services provided to all patients on a routine basis or to selected patients as needed.

This problem is directly associated with the second shortcoming of data on hospital prices: namely, it is even harder to measure the quantity of health care than to measure the quantity of most other goods and services. The content of a day in the hospital or of a visit to a physician's office depends sensitively on the equipment available to physicians and nurses and the stock of scientific knowledge that undergirds their actions. Both have grown prodigiously in recent decades. But not all of these new inputs are equally beneficial, and some may prove to be useless. This problem is important because the determination of changes in price hinges on the ability to measure quantities of output so that one can determine whether outlays have changed because of changes in quantities produced or because of changes in price.

Even if this problem were solved, many people would argue that the value of a unit of medical service cannot be identified apart from some measure of its value in improving health. But this step would require solid information about the efficacy of health care in bringing about particular physical or psychological outcomes and some set of weights for valuing these outcomes. Knowledge of the physical outcomes of medical interventions is extremely sparse, which has led the Department of Health and Human Services to initiate the major program of "outcomes" or "effectiveness" research described in chapter 3. Even this research, however, will not determine an appropriate set of weights to value these outcomes.

A third problem poses particularly serious obstacles to international comparisons. No objective valuation of health care services exists, because there is no market for many kinds of health care in most major nations, especially outside the United States. A similar problem arises in the United States with respect to services provided by government agencies, such as the Veterans Administration or the Indian Health Service, whose output is measured as budget cost. Whether expenditures of, say, $1 million by one of these agencies produce medical outputs equal to, larger than, or smaller than those produced by private payers or by the other agency is simply not known. In most other countries, hospitals operate under fixed budgets and physicians' fees or salaries are heavily influenced by political decisions. In the case of private outlays, the theory of consumer and producer behavior suggests that the last dollars spent on various commodities yield returns similar in general magnitude. No such presumption is justified when budgets are politically determined. If budgets are smaller than would be economically efficient, the marginal value of the publicly provided services exceeds that of private outlays. The reverse is true if budgets are larger than is socially optimal.

These problems are not unique to changes in health care spending. A 1990 automobile is not the same as a 1950 automobile. Efforts to determine how much investment changed during the 1980s are bedeviled by disputes about how computers should be valued (by the cost of computation or by the resources used in producing given computers) and hence about the rate at which the output of computers changed. No market exists for services of state universities and colleges. And the relative price of various commodities in general differs widely across nations. But these problems are particularly serious in the case of health care because the nature of the services rendered by health care providers is evolving so rapidly and the technology of health care differs widely from country to country. Furthermore, the relative remuneration of health care providers and the way health care delivery is organized differ enormously among different countries, as indicated above.

While some measurement problems apply to all commodities, the particular methods used in compiling official price statistics in the United States introduce additional distortions.[41] First, official price indices measure the cost per physician visit or hospital patient-day. Because of an increase in outpatient surgery, which is offered to patients who are less sick than the average hospital patient, the average cost of treating the remaining inpatients has increased. A cost-reducing innovation—the shift from inpatient to outpatient surgery—appears as a cost-increasing innovation. Second, official price indices measure fees charged to full-paying patients. Thus they take no account of the sharply increasing trend of insurers to negotiate

41. The following points are taken from Joseph P. Newhouse, "Measuring Medical Prices and Understanding Their Effects: The Baxter Foundation Prize Address," *Journal of Health Administration Education*, vol. 7 (Winter 1989), pp. 19–26.

discounts. Third, because hospital care is the largest single component of personal health care spending, it should be weighted more heavily in the construction of price indices than any other component of care. But the consumer price index weights various components of care on the basis of the out-of-pocket costs borne by consumers. Since individuals directly pay only about 5 percent of the cost of hospital care but most of the cost of dentistry and pharmaceutical products, hospital services are weighted less heavily than *either* dentistry or drugs—and yet total expenditures on hospital care are approximately three times larger than expenditures on dentists' services and drugs *combined*.

For all of these reasons, data on changes in health care prices within the United States are highly dubious. Efforts to compare health care prices across countries are also questionable.[42] Since such prices are necessary to measurement of real health care spending, the unreliability of price data means that one cannot confidently interpret health expenditures deflated by these price series as measures of the change in the quantity of real health care services over time or of differences across countries.

Other data that are more reliable than health care price series permit comparisons of the quantity of other goods and services that are forgone to provide health care. Specifically, information on nominal health expenditures at each point in time and on nominal gross national (or domestic) product are available, as are price series on gross national product that can be used to deflate nominal gross expenditures. Thus, data on the percentage of gross national (or domestic) product devoted to health care and deflators for gross national (or domestic) product can be used to compute changes over time within one country in the resource cost of health care services.

Such comparisons across countries remain treacherous, however. The problem in this case is that relative prices of the constituents of national income differ so considerably across countries that one can arrive at widely different judgments about the relative incomes in various countries depending on which set of prices is used. Thus comparisons of incomes in different countries are sometimes based

42. For a brief discussion of some of these issues, see "Health Care Expenditure and Other Data: An International Compendium from the Organization for Economic Cooperation and Development," *Health Care Financing Review, 1989 Annual Supplement*, pp. 114–15.

on exchange rates, which depend only on internationally traded goods and capital movements, and sometimes on the basis of "purchasing-power parity exchange rates," based on price indices representing a broad range of goods normally bought by households, whether traded internationally or not.

In the course of this book, I constructed time series of real expenditures on health care in the United States by deflating nominal health care spending by the gross national product deflator. This method provides a measure of the amounts of national product that U.S. households surrendered to buy health care services. It does not provide a reliable index of the quantity of health care services purchased at various times. For reasons stated above, I am not persuaded that real health expenditures calculated by deflating nominal outlays by health care price indices are reliable guides to changes in actual health care services.

In the case of international comparisons of levels of outlays, I present statistics that start with the fraction of gross domestic product devoted to health care services. Comparisons over time are based on the product of changes in that percentage and the growth of real gross domestic product. Once again, such series show changes in the resource cost of health care, not in the quantity of health care services provided. Comparisons across countries at a point in time are based on purchasing-power parity exchange rates. I have not used purchasing-power-equivalent health care prices as estimated by the Organization of Economic Cooperation and Development, because this series depends on market prices for a small proportion of total health care spending in countries where most health care services are not marketed.

Appendix B: Determinants of Health Care Spending

The equation used in note 29 appears below. It is estimated on data from the years 1986–88 for nineteen countries.

$$E = -5.35 + 0.11\,P + 1.40\,Y - 0.31\,S - 0.12\,D - 0.12\,NHS$$
$$\quad (-3.3) \quad (0.7) \quad (11.7) \quad (-1.7) \quad (-0.9) \quad (-1.3)$$
$$\bar{R}^2 = 0.90$$

where E is the logarithm of per capita health expenditures converted to U.S. dollars with purchasing-power parity exchange rates, P is the logarithm of population, Y is the logarithm of per capita gross domestic product converted to U.S. dollars with purchasing-power parity exchange rates, S is the logarithm of the share of public health care spending in total health care spending, D is a dummy variable for direct democracy in Switzerland, and NHS is a dummy variable for national health services in New Zealand and the United Kingdom. I used this functional form and these variables because I sought to replicate the equation used earlier by Leu. This equation omits a variable for urbanization used by Leu because the t-value is only 0.2. This equation implies that an increase in the U.S. public share from 41 percent to 100 percent would lower per capita outlays by 18 percent. The difference between these results and the earlier findings of Leu is consistent with the change in the stance of governments in many European countries from a policy of accommodating increases in health expenditures during the 1960s and 1970s to one of restricting growth of health care spending during the 1980s. It is also consistent with a less helpful explanation: that the estimating equation does not fully incorporate the various influences on health care spending and thus misstates the importance or effect of governments both in 1974 and in the late 1980s.

CHAPTER FIVE

The Terms of the Debate

THE UNITED STATES is beginning a major debate on the financing of health care. The major stakeholders in health care services—physicians and hospital administrators, management and labor, insurers, suppliers of equipment and pharmaceuticals, elected officials, and the general insured population—are becoming increasingly dissatisfied with the current system. For the debate to become serious, three conditions must be satisfied. The first is further deterioration in support for the current system, which rising costs, cost control efforts, and narrowing coverage make likely. The second is reduction in the federal budget deficit. A large deficit discourages any discussions of federal initiatives that might further widen it. The third condition is the determination by a president or presidential candidate to make reform of health care finance a central issue.

Elected officials and private organizations have already advanced many and varied plans to reform health care financing. These proposals differ primarily in the relative roles assigned to government and private organizations and in the comprehensiveness of the proposed changes. Some plans focus on acute care and its costs, while others encompass both acute and long-term care. The various options can be broadly categorized on the basis of how they address five major issues. Would the plan retain or replace the current system of employer-sponsored insurance for acute-care health services? If the plan would build on employer-sponsored insurance, would employers be encouraged or required to offer insurance? Would the plan institute major changes in the reimbursement of health care providers or build on current arrangements? Would the plan include coverage of home care and nursing home care? If the answer to the last question is yes, would the system depend on extension of private coverage or rely on public programs?

Because federal action in the immediate future seems unlikely, many states have moved to extend health insurance coverage and to control growth of spending. These initiatives may be the harbinger of a state-based approach to extending coverage and controlling costs. For reasons set forth below, state initiatives are more likely to act as laboratory models that will shape future federal action than to serve as the ultimate solution to current problems.

No simple categorization can capture all the dimensions of variation among the many plans recently advanced, but the plans tend to fall in one of three broad categories. The approach characterized below as "voluntary incrementalism" would try to perfect the current system of voluntary, employer-sponsored insurance and would broaden public programs for those outside the labor force. In some forms, generous refundable tax credits would assure virtually universal access to health care. It is the strategy embraced by those who oppose two more far-reaching reforms.

Under "mandatory employer-sponsored insurance," employers would be required to sponsor and pay for most of the cost of health insurance for all or most employees and their dependents, and employees would be obliged to accept such coverage. An extension of medicaid or a similar program would fill in coverage for virtually everyone else. A final group of plans, labeled "mandatory restructuring," would go beyond the requirement that employers sponsor health insurance for employees and would institute major changes in the way hospitals, physicians, and other providers are reimbursed.

Voluntary Incrementalism

Underlying voluntary incrementalism is the principle that many insurers should continue to offer diverse plans in order to provide choice among insurance plans, promote competition among insurers, and encourage innovation in methods of reimbursement of providers, which in turn can be used to hold down growth of costs in line with patient preferences.[1] Employers might be required to sponsor health insurance for their employees but not to pay for it.

Voluntary incrementalism aims to offer additional employees work-based health insurance by reducing or offsetting imperfections in the market for health insurance that make some plans prohibitively expensive and by providing tax subsidies to help low-income households afford health insurance. Such plans would provide increased access to medicaid benefits or other publicly subsidized care for those who lack access to employment-based insurance and are too poor to afford coverage on their own. They would rely on the development of private long-term care insurance that individuals would voluntarily buy on their own or through employers. And they would try to slow the growth of outlays by increasing competition in the market for health insurance and by encouraging such private regulatory devices as managed care. This approach minimizes the role of government in general and of mandates on private action in particular.

Risk Pools

Measures to increase the appeal of private insurance to companies that do not now offer it make up the centerpiece of voluntary incrementalism. "Risk pools," arrangements through which several small companies are treated as one large group for the purpose of setting premiums, would reduce or eliminate the surcharges that insurance companies add to premiums for small groups.[2] Public subsidies could be provided to such pools when the actual loss experience indicates abnormally high costs.

Tax credits for everyone would increase the affordability of private health insurance. If such credits covered virtually all costs of a basic health plan, the purchase of health insurance by individuals could be made mandatory. If the credit covered only a minor fraction of the cost, purchase of insurance would have to remain voluntary, but

1. Sponsors of plans belonging to the category of "voluntary incrementalism" include the Health Insurance Association of America, the U.S. Chamber of Commerce, the National Association of Manufacturers, the Manufacturers Alliance for Productivity and Innovation, Representative Willis D. Gradison, Jr., and Senator Orrin G. Hatch.

2. See Randall R. Bovbjerg, "Insuring the Uninsured through Private Action: Ideas and Initiatives," *Inquiry*, vol. 23 (Winter 1986), pp. 403–18.

the demand for it would increase in line with the drop in price. Because health costs vary widely, any given credit would cover different proportions of cost among regions and groups.

Experience to date offers little hope that such measures would result in coverage for most workers or members of their families who are now uninsured unless the government provided large subsidies.[3] If subsidies to employers were large enough to induce substantially universal coverage of workers and their families, employers who currently offer insurance would be tempted to drop it and join the pools, thus greatly boosting budgetary costs and defeating the private-market focus of the approach.[4]

Tax Credits

Supporters of voluntary incrementalist reforms of health care financing typically favor changes in tax policy to extend health insurance and increase cost consciousness. Some support refundable tax credits to make health insurance affordable for everyone. For the same reason, many support limiting or completely eliminating the exclusion of health insurance premiums from personal income tax.[5]

Large refundable tax credits would cause almost everyone to buy insurance. This approach poses a dilemma usually encountered in

3. Katherine Swartz with the assistance of Debra Lipson, "Strategies for Assisting the Medically Indigent and People without Health Insurance," Urban Institute Working Paper 3785-02 (Washington, January 1989); and Katherine Swartz with the assistance of Debra Lipson, *Strategies for Assisting the Medically Uninsured* (Washington: Urban Institute, 1989).

4. Martin Holmer estimates that the price elasticity of demand for health insurance ranges between −0.39 for families with gross incomes in 1979 of less than $15,000 (equivalent to about $26,000 in 1990) to −0.06 for families with 1979 incomes above $40,000 (equivalent to $70,000 in 1990). "Tax Policy and the Demand for Health Insurance," *Journal of Health Economics*, vol. 3 (December 1984), pp. 203–21. In 1986, 30.6 million members of families with annual incomes of less than $20,000 had private health insurance, while 23 million were uninsured through any plan. According to Holmer's estimates, cutting the price of health insurance in half, through a tax credit or any other means, would increase the number with insurance by about 20 percent ($0.5 \times 0.39 = 0.195$), which would bring insurance to about 6 million of the 23 million uninsured.

5. An early proponent of changing the tax system to promote reform of health care financing is Alain C. Enthoven, *Health Plan: The Only Practical Solution to the Soaring Cost of Medical Care* (Addison-Wesley, 1980).

the field of cash welfare policy. If credits are available to everyone regardless of income, they will transfer a major part of the cost of personal health care services (more than $600 billion in 1991) onto public budgets. Such a policy would require enormous tax increases.[6]

If the subsidy were reduced as income increases, millions of people would face sharply higher implicit tax rates arising from the reduction in the credit. The cost of health insurance coverage for a family of four could easily run $4,000 annually.[7] If the family were entitled to a $4,000 credit that was reduced by, say, 20 percent of annual family income above $5,000, all four-person families with annual incomes below $25,000 would face an additional "tax" of 20 percent. Combined with payroll taxes of 15.3 percent, personal income taxes that start at 15 percent, and state income taxes, millions of four-person families would face taxes of at least 50 percent. If the tax credit were reduced more slowly as income rises, the number of people eligible for subsidy and the cost of the subsidies would both increase. If the tax credit were reduced faster, then the tax rate would rise and pose even larger work disincentives for those affected.[8]

Part of any cost of liberalized tax credits could be offset by increased revenues from limitation or repeal of the current exclusion of employer-sponsored insurance, which reduces federal revenues by $36 billion in 1991.[9] With a liberal, refundable credit, the exclusion of employer-financed health insurance premiums from personal tax would cease to have any rationale because employers would stop paying such premiums. If tax credits do not provide far larger benefits than those from the current exclusion, many employers will refuse

6. The Heritage Foundation proposes a refundable tax credit of 20 percent, but the plan is not voluntary as it would require individuals to buy insurance. This plan holds down the proportion of health care costs that shows up on government budgets. It also provides a large windfall to businesses that now pay for health insurance for their workers and families, but does so by shifting insurance costs directly to household budgets.

7. The employer cost of health insurance per worker in 1989 averaged $2,853 but exceeded $4,000 in many major industries (chemicals and allied products; rubber, leather, and plastic products; transportation equipment; public utilities). These costs exclude employee-paid premiums and increases since 1989. See U.S. Chamber Research Center, *Employee Benefits: Survey Data from Benefit Year 1989, 1990 Edition* (Washington: U.S. Chamber of Commerce, 1990), p. 14.

8. This issue was first posed by Christopher Green, *Negative Taxes and the Poverty Problem* (Brookings, 1967).

9. *Budget of the United States Government, Fiscal Year 1992*, table XI-1, p. 3-36.

to sponsor insurance plans unless forced to do so and many workers will refuse to accept coverage unless acceptance is mandatory. But such credits would place a heavy burden on the federal budget.

Medicaid Extension

Extension of medicaid eligibility to some groups not currently covered by the program is a third element of voluntary incrementalism. Because no employment-based system can reach members of households with no one in the labor force and with incomes too low to support health insurance benefits, this mandatory component of the program is needed to guarantee essentially universal coverage within a system that relies predominantly on voluntary actions of businesses and individuals.

Medicaid or a similar program could underwrite subsidies to enable individuals or employers to buy medicaid coverage at a price scaled to family income. This approach completely circumvents the administrative difficulties and costs of forming risk pools for low-wage workers and incorporates an individually tailored subsidy.

Medicaid "buy-ins" create a potentially serious problem, however. If the subsidy is small, few employers or individuals are likely to buy coverage. If it is large enough to induce employers to buy in to medicaid, some employers who now offer wholly private plans will be tempted to drop them and transfer their employees to medicaid. Such an approach would shift health care costs from private budgets to public budgets and would cause shifts among companies in gross costs of hiring workers.

The cost of extending medicaid coverage to all of the poor depends on the number of poor people not covered by medicaid or employer-sponsored insurance. In 1989, for example, the public cost of expanding medicaid to all those with incomes below official poverty thresholds would have been about $9 billion if all employees had been covered by employer-sponsored health insurance. If the medicaid extensions contained in the Omnibus Reconciliation Act of 1990 had been fully implemented, the cost of covering the rest of the poor would have been only about $7 billion. Without workplace insurance, the cost rises to more than $13 billion to cover those now without insurance. If medicaid provided all coverage for the poor, the added cost would run from $22 billion to $30 billion.[10] The full costs of extending medicaid almost certainly are much larger, as sizable increases in the fees medicaid pays physicians would be necessary in many states to induce a sufficient number of physicians to serve an expanded medicaid population.

Long-Term Care

The voluntary incrementalist approach to long-term care would count on private insurers to develop plans that most individuals or businesses would buy. Private insurance currently pays for only about 1 percent of long-term care.

Such insurance has attracted little interest among young workers for whom the prospects of disability are remote. Of those who reach age 65, an estimated 43 percent will enter a nursing home, 24 percent will stay one year or more, and 9 percent will stay five years or more.[11] It is hardly surprising that young workers prefer cash wages or other fringe benefits to insurance against such unpleasant and remote risks. For older people, the risk is more immediate, but the cost of good insurance is very high.[12]

Despite these problems, the large potential size of the market for long-term care insurance has led companies to devote considerable

10. Kenneth E. Thorpe and Joanna E. Siegel, "Covering the Uninsured: Interactions among Public and Private Sector Strategies," *Journal of the American Medical Association*, October 20, 1989, pp. 2114–18; and John Holahan and Sheila Zedlewski, "Insuring Low-Income Americans: Is Medicaid the Answer?" Urban Institute Working Paper 3836-03 (Washington, July 1990).

11. Peter Kemper and Christopher Murtaugh, "Lifetime Use of Nursing Home Care," *New England Journal of Medicine*, February 28, 1991, pp. 595–600.

12. Costs of insurance depend sensitively on such factors as the age of the insured, the size of deductibles, the number of years of protection, and the presence or absence of indexing. Rates for 77-year-olds are more than twice those for 62-year-olds. Indexing of benefits more than triples premiums for 50-year-olds and more than doubles them for 65-year-olds. A plan with unlimited coverage costs about twice as much as a plan with a two-year maximum. A plan that provides $60 a day, increased 5.5 percent a year as an inflation offset, and offers unlimited benefits after a sixty-day deductible costs an estimated $2,657 a year for a 67-year-old and $5,560 for an 82-year-old. See Joshua M. Wiener, Katherine M. Harris, and Raymond J. Hanley, *Premium Pricing of Prototype Private Long-Term Care Insurance Policies*, Final Report to the Office of the Assistant Secretary for Planning and Evaluation/Social Services Policy of the U.S. Department of Health and Human Services, Brookings, December 1990. Because insurers know that they cannot accurately estimate future long-term care prices or lapse rates among the insured, they set prices even higher than these estimated costs.

resources to designing and marketing new plans. Prospects are good that insurance companies, working in cooperation with employers, can eventually design plans that will appeal to a significant proportion of the population. These prospects would be enhanced if tax laws were modified so that the investment yield on reserves accumulated in such plans were exempt from tax until benefits were paid, as under private pension plans,[13] and they would be greatly enhanced if the federal government offered direct subsidies to people judged too poor to buy insurance.

Without large subsidies, voluntarily purchased private insurance cannot credibly promise anything approaching universal coverage for long-term care. Projections indicate that even with large subsidies no more than roughly half the population would eventually purchase long-term-care insurance.[14] The other half or more of the population either would remain uninsured or would require coverage under some form of income-tested government program, such as medicaid. Coverage of only part of the population would result in high selling costs and other administrative expenses associated with private insurance. It would also leave millions uninsured or dependent on an income- or means-tested program.

Competition

Promotion of competition to help slow the growth of health care spending is a fourth component of voluntary incrementalism. Encouraging price consciousness in the purchase of both health insurance and medical care is one way to foster competition among insurers and providers. The complete exclusion of employer-financed insurance from personal income tax reduces price consciousness because it spares individuals the taxes they must pay on other earnings. These tax rules boost the amount of health insurance people want, and increased insurance in turn raises consumption of health services. For this reason, taxation of health insurance premiums

13. On the assumption that proceeds would be used to cover costs of long-term care that would be deductible under the personal income tax over some threshold fraction of income, these benefits would be substantially tax exempt.

14. Robert M. Ball with Thomas N. Bethell, *Because We're All in This Together* (Washington: Families U.S.A. Foundation, 1989); and Alice M. Rivlin and Joshua M. Wiener with Raymond J. Hanley and Denise A. Spence, *Caring for the Disabled Elderly: Who Will Pay?* (Brookings, 1988).

beyond a certain level remains a key element of voluntary incremen-talism. It is hoped that employees' willingness to accept cost-decreasing elements of health insurance—such as higher cost sharing and managed care—would be fostered if the cost of refusing such provisions began to show up as taxable income.[15]

Competition can also be promoted by offering improved information about providers' prices and quality of services. The Health Care Financing Administration (HCFA) has begun to publish mortality rates and other data on hospital performance. The publication of similar data on physicians is under discussion. The practical questions are whether such data validly measure the quality of care and whether businesses, insurance companies, and individuals will be able to use such information to buy care of a given quality at least cost. Valid measures do not yet exist of the complexity of various cases that are classified under a given diagnostic category. Without such measures one cannot tell whether a hospital with higher than average costs per case or above-average mortality rates is operating inefficiently or is receiving sicker than average patients.

Competition among insurance companies offers yet another way of controlling expenditures. In addition to providing underwriting and claims processing, insurance companies now offer to help employer-sponsors to manage care. While managed care has resulted in some savings through case management, preadmission certification, utilization review, mandatory second opinions, and other devices, these savings are primarily one-time reductions: once achieved, they cannot be replicated. These cost control measures themselves use up resources, and only a minority of companies think that they have been effective. Furthermore, no slowdown in total health care spending is detectable over the period when managed care has come into widespread use.[16]

How much increased competition is likely to reduce cost is unclear. Advocates of increased competition claim that large sustainable

15. The effect of denying the tax exclusion would be to force employees to pay a price for extra coverage equal to the taxes charged on the newly taxable portion of health insurance premiums.

16. William B. Schwartz, "The Inevitable Failure of Current Cost-Containment Strategies: Why They Can Provide Only Temporary Relief," *Journal of the American Medical Association*, January 9, 1987, pp. 220–24; and William B. Schwartz and Daniel N. Mendelson, "Hospital Cost Containment in the 1980s: Hard Lessons Learned and Prospects for the 1990s," *New England Journal of Medicine*, April 11, 1991, pp. 1037–42.

savings are feasible. Large initial savings may be possible and are worth seeking. But the long-term slowdown in spending is likely to be modest because competition can only modestly attenuate the primary force behind the rise in health care outlays, the development of new methods of diagnosis and treatment. Competition will deter some patients from seeking some fraction of low-benefit care in the whole range of extant medical interventions. It will also encourage providers to produce services with heightened efficiency. But unless the stream of innovations slowed, the principal force behind the long-run increase in outlays would persist. To be sure, major constraints on the demand for health care are likely to eventually slow innovation. However, any effects on innovation would take many years to be felt because the gestation of most medical innovations is long, and many costly medical advances are on the verge of introduction.[17]

Advantages and Disadvantages

Voluntary incrementalism would require no major breaks with current policy. This is its strength and its weakness. Improvements in the operation of insurance markets would extend coverage to some uninsured groups. Increased competition would somewhat reduce the growth of spending. Vigorous marketing will increase sales of long-term care insurance.

But this strategy holds out little hope for eliminating the gaps in acute-care health insurance unless it includes large tax credits that would shift privately financed outlays to public budgets. Nor will it slow the growth of costs as much as would be economically and socially desirable or provide financial access to long-term care for most people. The extension of private insurance through risk pools or other devices has done little so far to spread employment-based insurance for acute care. Medicaid extensions can cover only about one-sixth of the uninsured, even if they reach everyone officially designated as poor. If medicaid is extended to people with incomes well above poverty thresholds, it reduces incentives for private employers to offer ordinary plans. Private insurance companies are

17. For a short list of already developed high-cost innovations, see Henry J. Aaron and William B. Schwartz, "Rationing Health Care: The Choice before Us," *Science*, January 26, 1990, pp. 418–22.

trying hard, but so far with little success, to design long-term-care insurance plans that will appeal to large numbers of employees and employers.

Increased competition holds out the prospect of shaving at most 5 to 10 percent off hospital and physician outlays, with the saving spread over several years.[18] In view of the huge size of health care outlays, the resulting savings could run to as much as $40 billion (in 1990 prices). Such savings would be impressive and clearly a great boon. However, because they would be spread out over many years, they might be hard to detect against the background increase in real outlays, currently running about $25 billion a year. Potential savings are likely to be much smaller, because part of the possible economies have already been achieved since the advent of the diagnosis related group system, preferred provider organizations, and managed care.

Mandatory Employment-Based Insurance

Mandatory employment-based insurance, like voluntary incrementalism, would build upon, rather than replace, the current employment-based insurance system.[19] In contrast to voluntary incrementalism, it would legally compel employers to sponsor and pay most of the cost of private insurance or to support public coverage by paying a tax. Underlying the willingness to use government power is the conviction that incentives will not suffice to encourage the voluntary extension of acute health care unless large subsidies shift to public budgets much of the cost of health care that is now privately financed. Like voluntary incrementalism, this approach would extend medicaid or introduce some similar government program to cover people outside families with an employed member. It could

18. This crude estimate is based on studies of the difference in costs for hospital care and physician services between staff-model health maintenance organizations and fee-for-service medicine. The implicit assumption is that competition could reduce costs by no more than that difference.

19. Mandatory employment-based insurance has been advocated by the American Medical Association, the National Leadership Commission on Health Care, the U.S. Bipartisan Commission for Comprehensive Health Care (the Pepper Commission), Senator Edward M. Kennedy and Representative Henry A. Waxman (H.R. 1845 in 1989), the Foundation of American Health Systems, the American Academy of Pediatrics, and former California Governor George Deukmajian.

use various methods to control the growth of expenditures and develop coverage for long-term care. It could be combined with the competitive strategy sketched above and with reliance on markets to provide private long-term care insurance. But the mandatory approach to acute-care coverage is consistent intellectually and politically with direct government regulation of provider charges and with a prominent role for government in ensuring coverage for long-term care.

Description

Under this approach, employers would be required either to sponsor and pay most of the cost of acute-care health insurance for all employees who work more than a minimum number of hours and for their dependents, or pay a tax instead if they refuse to offer such coverage (sometimes called "play or pay"). The tax typically is set high enough to cause most employers to offer insurance, but low enough so that certain employers could elect to pay the penalty instead. The plans typically limit the proportion of the total premium that employees can be required to pay. Those not covered by employer-sponsored plans would be insured under a backup public plan, paid for by the proceeds of the tax paid by employers who opt not to sponsor plans, along with other revenues.

Employers electing to pay the tax rather than offer insurance would include those exposed to unusually high premiums or having abnormally low wage levels. Employers could be denied the option of paying the tax instead of sponsoring insurance, but only if experience rating were eliminated or if public subsidies insulated employers from the full brunt of above-average premiums.

Perhaps the most important issue to be resolved under mandatory employer-sponsored plans concerns the criteria used to determine the population covered by workplace insurance versus that of the backup plan. At least four alternatives are available.[20] First, responsibility for households with incomes below a specified threshold—some multiple of the poverty threshold, for example—could be left to the public plan through direct coverage or subsidies to private

20. This categorization is taken from Lynn Etheredge, "Toward a New Public-Private Partnership for the Uninsured," Washington, July 1990.

employers who would cover the poor. Second, employers' financial responsibility could be limited to a fixed proportion of payroll costs. Third, the financial responsibility of employer-sponsored plans could be restricted to health care expenses below some "stop-loss" limit; larger charges would be covered by some form of public "reinsurance." In the same general category, employers could be protected from high experience-rated premiums by public subsidy. Finally, public coverage might be limited to particular groups—children and pregnant women, for example—while private insurance continued as under current arrangements or under a mandate. To minimize reliance on a new backup plan, medicare would be retained.

The purpose of all of these limits on employer responsibility is to hold down the number of employers who face very large increases in employment costs. Employers paying very low average wages or operating dangerous establishments or communities with unusually high medical costs could face short-run increases in medical costs large enough to undermine business survival. While standard economic analysis suggests that these costs will eventually be reflected in lower wages than would otherwise have been paid or higher prices than would otherwise have been charged, these adjustments take time, during which employers who cannot shift these added costs to their customers would face reduced profits. These adjustment problems would be especially serious for businesses that employ casual or low-skill labor and that have elected not to sponsor health insurance. Accordingly, such companies—fast-food establishments, for example—find mandatory employer-sponsored insurance adverse to their private interests.

Mandatory employment-based insurance plans must resolve a large number of additional issues.[21]

—Which employers should be required to participate? For example, should small companies or the self-employed be included or excluded?

—Should premiums be uniform across all employers nationally or regionally, or reflect the actual claims experience of each group?

21. For an exhaustive and informative examination of these issues, see *Insuring the Uninsured: Options and Analysis,* Committee Print, Subcommittee on Labor-Management Relations and Subcommittee on Labor Standards of the House Committee on Education and Labor, Subcommittee on Health and the Environment of House

—Which workers should be included? Should only full-time workers be included, and if so, how many hours a week should an employer have to work to be considered full time?

—Should employee participation be voluntary or mandatory for themselves and for their dependents when employers pay only part of the premium?

—How much cost sharing should be imposed on those who are insured? Should there be caps on deductibles or total payments per patient or per family?

—What agency should be charged with enforcing the mandate—a federal agency, states, or some newly constituted organization?

—What penalties should be imposed for violation of plan requirements?

Illustrative Plans

Two plans illustrate mandatory coverage for acute care. The National Leadership Commission on Health Care (NLC) has proposed that all employers be required to sponsor and pay at least three-quarters of the cost of a health insurance plan offering a defined set of benefits to every employee aged 18 or older who worked more than twenty-five hours a week and to that employee's dependents.[22] Companies that failed to offer such a plan would be required to pay a tax of about 9 percent of earnings up to the limit taxable under social security ($53,400 in 1991).[23] Whether companies sponsored insurance for full-time workers or paid the tax, they would have to pay the tax on behalf of uncovered part-time employees. Cost sharing by patients could not exceed $1,000 annually per patient ($3,000 per family). Employers could offer more generous plans if they wished.

Anyone not covered by an employment-based plan (including those eligible for medicaid acute-care benefits) would be covered by a new universal-access program offering the same benefits as the employment-based plan. People with incomes above 150 percent of

Committee on Energy and Commerce, and Senate Special Committee on Aging, 100 Cong. 2 sess. (Government Printing Office, October 1988), p. 109.

22. National Leadership Commission on Health Care, *For the Health of a Nation: A Shared Responsibility* (Ann Arbor, Mich.: Health Administration Press Perspectives, 1989).

23. The limit on taxable earnings in 1988, the year for which the NLC did its cost estimates, was $48,000.

official poverty thresholds would be required to pay a tax of about 2 to $2\frac{1}{2}$ percent of earnings for coverage, whether or not they had employment-based coverage. The proceeds of this tax, together with current government expenditures on medicaid, would finance insurance for everyone not covered under employment-based plans.

Hawaii took a different approach in 1974 when it required employers to sponsor health insurance plans that provide a basic package of health benefits for employees (other than seasonal workers or real estate and insurance agents) who work at least twenty hours a week and have been employed for four weeks.[24] The requirement does not extend to the dependents of workers. The required services included up to 120 days of hospitalization, surgery and anesthesia, physicians' services, diagnostic laboratory and X-ray services, and maternity services. Employers are required to pay at least half the cost of these services, but employees cannot be required to pay more than 1.5 percent of wages. After initial opposition from some employer groups and some insurers, who feared government regulation, the program has gained general acceptance.

The history of the Hawaii plan illustrates the power of the Employee Retirement Income Security Act of 1974 (ERISA). ERISA exempts self-insured plans from state regulation. Citing ERISA, the Chevron Corporation successfully sued to block enforcement of the Hawaii plan. Congress enacted a special exemption for the Hawaii plan in 1981, but stipulated that the exemption referred only to services listed in the original plan, thus preventing Hawaii from requiring self-insured plans to include other services (mental health and substance abuse prevention, for example) that the state mandated for plans sold by commercial insurers.

In 1989 Hawaii added a state health insurance program to the mandatory employment-based arrangement and to medicaid. The purpose was to reach as many as possible of the 5 percent of the population that remained uncovered. This plan provided a lean set of benefits (up to five days of hospitalization, maternity care, childhood immunizations, and certain other primary care benefits). The plan requires premium payments by those with incomes over official

24. Jack Hadley and Judith Miller Jones, "Expanding Access to Health Care in the States: Experimenting with Mandates in Hawaii and Massachusetts," Issue Brief no. 555, George Washington University, National Health Policy Forum (Washington, 1990).

poverty thresholds and limited copayments. People who are outside the labor force or exempted from the employment-based system are eligible.

These plans provide a higher fraction of the residents of Hawaii with health coverage than those of any other state. Per capita costs of care are about average, suggesting that near-universal coverage does not necessarily result in either inflation or effective control on the growth of costs.

Both the NLC and the Hawaii plans aim for nearly universal coverage. Even without a backup plan for those not covered through work, universal employment-based insurance would extend coverage to more than fourth-fifths of the currently uninsured if employees working at least ten hours a week for a single employer were covered and if they were required to accept coverage offered to them.[25] These plans or others of the same genre would sharply reduce the number of "gaps" in the current system—waiting periods for new employees, exclusions for previous conditions, and holes in coverage.[26]

Cost Control

Mandatory insurance heightens concern about cost control. Because such coverage would increase demand, many fear that it would exacerbate inflation. Furthermore, proposals to mandate

25. *Cost and Effects of Extending Health Insurance Coverage*, Committee Print, Subcommittee on Labor-Management Relations and Subcommittee on Labor Standards of House Committee on Education and Labor, Subcommittee on Health and the Environment of House Committee on Energy and Commerce, and Senate Special Committee on Aging, 100 Cong. 2 sess. (GPO, October 1988), p. 73.

26. Alvin L. Schorr argues that job turnover poses an insuperable barrier to universal coverage under employer-sponsored insurance in "Job Turnover—A Problem with Employer-based Health Care," *New England Journal of Medicine*, August 23, 1990, pp. 543–45. The reasons he advances are unpersuasive, however. The administrative problems of assuring continuous coverage during transitions are easily solved for most workers under current arrangements and could be handled universally with standardized rules. Disqualification for coverage because of preexisting conditions cannot be a problem because the essence of mandatory employer-sponsored plans must be the prohibition of such disqualifications. Finally, while some families might choose to leave dependents uninsured if dependent coverage were optional, as Schorr fears, mandatory employer-sponsored plans can easily incorporate the requirement that employees must elect coverage for dependents who are not eligible for the public backup plan.

employment-based coverage and to cover others through a backup plan are consistent with virtually any approach to the problem of rising medical costs.

The NLC, for example, advocated that state agencies responsible for those not covered by employer plans negotiate with providers over fees. But the NLC left open the question of whether these agencies should also be empowered to set fees used under employer-sponsored insurance. The commission suggested that the state agencies might wish to use PPOs or HMOs to hold down costs, but it did not recommend any structural change in the fee-for-service method of reimbursing hospitals and physicians. Considerable doubts exist over whether the controls proposed by the NLC would effectively hold down costs unless these controls were buttressed by direct limits on the budgets of hospitals and restrictions on the range of services that can be provided outside the hospital setting (and hence outside the budget limits). The central problem is that the extension of health insurance aggravates the problem endemic under any insurance plan: patients and providers face little cost at time of care and hence have the incentive to seek and dispense services whose benefits are small relative to cost.

Several plans to impose direct limits on the growth of hospital spending have been advanced since rising health costs have become a matter of public concern. During phase II of the price control program implemented during the Nixon administration, Congress imposed limits on the growth of hospital revenues per patient-day that held down costs briefly, but these proved administratively cumbersome and were abandoned. Real hospital spending rose sharply thereafter. The Carter administration proposed to cap total annual hospital revenues and to discourage admissions by adjusting the cap less than proportionately for changes in caseloads. Congress rejected the Carter plan after hospitals vowed to control costs through a "voluntary effort," which proved to be utterly ineffectual. The DRG system implemented in 1984 excluded states that operated hospital cost control programs that promised savings at least as large as those expected from the DRG system. One state (Maryland) is now exempt. In 1984 Senator Edward M. Kennedy and Representative Richard A. Gephardt proposed state controls on growth of hospital spending and federal government controls if states did not meet minimum standards. None of these plans has come near passage, and no recent administration has shown any interest in expanding direct controls.

Long-Term Care

Although it would be possible to require employers to offer their workers long-term care insurance and to pay for some part of the premium cost, no such major proposal has been advanced. The reason is quite straightforward: private long-term care insurance lacks wide market appeal. It simply has not ranked high on the wish lists of either workers or their employers.

Group long-term-care insurance suffers from other problems whose solution might detract from its appeal. Indexed long-term-care benefits not likely to be consumed for decades would be costly.[27] The tax concessions that might increase the appeal of long-term-care insurance have the same effect on budgetary balance as direct expenditures do and should be weighed against other measures to extend coverage for long-term care. In particular, unless all employees were included in such a plan or strict measures ensured that coverage for long-term care would be extended to low- and moderate-income households, much of the lost revenue would simply be a tax cut for upper-income households, many of whom would be able to pay for long-term care anyway.

Advantages and Disadvantages

Mandatory employer-sponsored coverage has the potential to extend health insurance to roughly five out of six of currently uninsured Americans. In combination with liberalization of medicaid or some other public backup plan, it could achieve virtually universal coverage. Unless it were combined with administrative controls over total payments to physicians and hospitals, however, it would increase health care costs not only by the value of the added services con-

27. Wiener and others, *Premium Pricing of Prototype Private Long-Term Care Insurance Policies,* table 4. An unindexed plan costs less than one-fourth as much as an indexed plan for this age group. But without indexation, 5.5 percent inflation reduces the real value of a $60 daily benefit to $7.05 if a 40-year-old worker does not claim benefits until he or she is 80 years old.

sumed by those who are now uninsured but by additional amounts caused by inflation in health care costs for all.

Furthermore, requiring employers to sponsor and finance insurance would add a fixed sum—the mandated premium—to the cost of hiring workers. Standard economic theory holds that either of two results would follow. For workers paid well above the minimum wage, the growth of money wages or other fringe benefits would be slowed until, eventually, lower money wages or other fringes would offset the added insurance costs. For workers paid at or near the minimum wage, the statutory wage floor would prevent this offset from occurring. Employers would be discouraged from hiring and might lay off some low-wage workers. Furthermore, the adjustment in wages for other workers would not happen instantly. During the transition, employers compelled to add insurance would experience increased costs that would cut into profits or force price increases and might threaten business survival in some cases. For these reasons, most programs for requiring employer-sponsored insurance either allow companies to elect to pay a tax instead of offering insurance or offer transitional subsidies to companies whose costs would be disproportionately increased.

More fundamentally, mandating health benefits would extend government rules over yet another aspect of the operation of private businesses. Many such rules now exist. Employers must pay taxes to support social security, medicare, and unemployment insurance. They must buy insurance to compensate workers for employment-related injuries. Federal rules require that workplaces meet federally established standards for health and safety. Employers once fought all of these taxes and rules as infringements of management prerogatives. Employers, most of whom behave responsibly, resent government regulations that infringe their freedom to make what they regard as ordinary business decisions. One might dismiss resistance to mandatory health insurance as just another rearguard action by employers in the war to maintain as much freedom as possible to manage their businesses as they see fit. But business executives are concerned that the federal government, confronting intractable budget deficits and unwilling to raise taxes or cut other spending, will force business to provide services that elected officials refuse to fund directly.

Furthermore, internal conflicts on health care financing divide the business community. Businesses that do not pay any insurance premiums are now free-riding on hidden subsidies. First, many of their employees are covered by insurance earned by other family members employed by businesses that pay for all or part of family coverage. Second, because some workers or their dependents are covered by medicaid, companies that do not offer insurance are subsidized by the general taxpayer. Third, other employees not covered by employment-based insurance receive uncompensated care, the cost of which physicians and hospitals recover by boosting charges of insured patients.[28]

These financial flows provoke two different responses. Opponents of mandatory employer-sponsored say that, if health insurance is a national priority, government should collect taxes and finance it, rather than imposing this responsibility on employers.[29] Supporters reply that the United States is heavily committed to employer-sponsored health insurance, which could be extended less disruptively than it can be replaced. They hold that imposing taxes sufficient to finance universal insurance publicly is politically impossible.[30] And, if employer-sponsored insurance is to continue, they ask why companies that offer insurance should have to continue providing implicit subsidies to companies that do not.

Comprehensive Restructuring

Comprehensive restructuring of the U.S. health insurance system can follow either of two courses: replacing employer-sponsored plans with government-sponsored insurance, or modifying employer-

28. Frank A. Sloan, *Uncompensated Medical Care: Rights and Responsibilities* (Johns Hopkins University Press, 1986).

29. Uwe E. Reinhardt, "Should All Employers Be Required by Law to Provide Basic Health Insurance Coverage for Their Employees and Dependents?" in Employee Benefit Research Institute, *Government Mandating of Employee Benefits* (Washington, 1987), pp. 121–33.

30. Furthermore, the financing of mandated benefits causes smaller distortion of economic behavior than taxes used to finance government provision if premiums are regarded by both employers and employees as a "benefit tax." A benefit tax is one that, like market price, is closely matched to perceived benefit. See Lawrence H. Summers, "Some Simple Economics of Mandated Benefits," *American Economic Review*, vol. 79 (May 1989, *Papers and Proceedings, 1988*), pp. 177–83.

sponsored insurance to achieve both universal coverage and effective budget control over health care providers.

Government-Sponsored Insurance

For more than two decades, various plans have called for the replacement of employment-based health insurance with direct government provision of health insurance as an attribute of citizenship or residence.[31] Each citizen or resident would receive a health card or would otherwise be assured access to a specified list of services. The cost of such services would be supported by some combination of taxes on individuals and businesses and reallocation of public funds from programs that the new comprehensive plan would replace. Although some critics liken this approach to the British National Health Service, under which physicians either work for salary in government-operated hospitals or are paid on a per capita basis, few U.S. advocates of government-sponsored insurance call for government employment of physicians.

The replacement of the current system by a wholly new one promises important benefits of truly universal coverage. It also holds the maximum potential for cutting administrative expenses and for gaining leverage over health costs, since a single authority would determine physicians' fees and hospital budgets.[32] Whether the promise would be realized is unclear: would the political system control providers, or would providers capture the political regulatory system for their own ends?[33]

31. Current supporters include the Health Security Action Council and the Committee for National Health Insurance, two groups sponsored by labor unions; Physicians for a National Health Program, a Boston-based group of physicians; and Representatives Marty Russo and Fortney H. (Pete) Stark, Jr. For a description of past plans, see Karen Davis, *National Health Insurance: Benefits, Costs, and Consequences* (Brookings, 1975). The most sweeping of these plans, the Health Security Act cosponsored by Senator Edward M. Kennedy and former Representative Martha Griffiths, would have provided tax-financed health care to everyone without cost sharing.

32. The costs of a new government bureaucracy would be considerable, but they would be more than offset by the savings from reduced private bureaucracy. Large savings would arise from replacing many payers with one. See David U. Himmelstein and Steffie Woolhandler, "Cost without Benefit: Administrative Waste in U.S. Health Care," *New England Journal of Medicine*, February 13, 1986, pp. 441–45.

33. Sam Peltzman, "The Economic Theory of Regulation after a Decade of Deregulation," *Brookings Papers on Economic Activity, Microeconomics, 1989*, pp. 1–41. As

THE CANADIAN SYSTEM.   In recent years, the Canadian system of paying for health care has become an object of considerable interest in the United States. The various Canadian provinces operate separate plans for paying for health care. All must meet certain national standards, but they differ in detail. In general, patients receive care without charge, hospitals operate on fixed budgets, and physicians are paid on a fee-for-service basis according to a fee schedule set by the province. If total outlays exceed targets, the fees are reduced in later years to hold spending to the desired level. Physicians cannot charge more than this fee and hence cannot bill patients for any excess over the scheduled fee. Efforts to control rising costs have led to complaints about the deterioration of services—queues, insufficient equipment, and denial of care.[34] Despite these difficulties, public opinion polls indicate that Canadians think their system is superior to that of either the United States or the United Kingdom and that Americans also think the Canadian system compares favorably with their own.

OBSTACLES TO GOVERNMENT-SPONSORED PLANS.   Two characteristics of plans to shift financing from the workplace to public budgets have prevented them from ever being taken seriously in Congress. First, they would shift hundreds of billions of dollars of expenditures from private to public budgets with associated increases in taxes. To be sure, the increase in public costs would be offset somewhat by reductions in income tax deductions for insurance premiums, and reduced private spending on private health insurance and health care would largely offset the tax increases necessary to pay for public benefits. In fact, net savings from enhanced cost control might eventually lower the total cost of health care, according to advocates. But many groups—including physicians, hospitals, and pharmaceutical com-

---

noted in chapter 4, governments of other countries play a much larger part in the management of the health care system than is true in the United States, and they have experienced slower growth of health care spending. But slower growth of medical spending abroad may be attributable to factors other than governmental involvement. And even if governments abroad have been instrumental in slowing growth of expenditures, the United States might not realize similar economies because the U.S. political system differs from those abroad.

34. John K. Igelhart, "Canada's Health System," *New England Journal of Medicine*, July 17, September 18, and December 18, 1986, pp. 202–08, 778–841, 1623–28; and Igelhart, "Canada's Health Care System Faces Its Problems," *New England Journal of Medicine*, February 22, 1990, pp. 562–68.

panies—are threatened by such proposals. And opponents would decry the shift as a radical extension of government power.

Second, a fully national health plan would abruptly end jobs of tens of thousands of private workers responsible for the administration of current plans in insurance companies and other private businesses. It would require massive reorganization of methods of payment. And it would reduce private control over health insurance plans. Such an upheaval seems to many too high a price to pay for extending insurance to the minority of uninsured Americans and for speculative claims of improved cost control, particularly if significant progress toward these objectives can be made with less disruptive reforms.

Universal Coverage and Payment Reform

Comprehensive restructuring does not really require the transfer of all payment responsibility from private to public budgets. The essence of such reform is a combination of two elements: reforms in the insurance net, so that essentially all people are protected almost all of the time against the financial risks of illness; and reforms in the ways physicians, hospitals, and other providers are paid, to curb the tendency under current insurance arrangements to provide large amounts of low-benefit, high-cost care.

THE NEW YORK PLAN. The Department of Health of the State of New York published a draft plan (UNY*Care) in 1989 to establish mandatory employment-based health insurance that would have gone beyond simple mandates in two key respects.[35] It proposed to create a state-managed "single-payer authority" that would collect payments for health services from private insurers, set rates of reimbursement for all providers, and pay providers. The authority would determine whether providers should be reimbursed on a fee-for-service basis, under a fixed budget, or on a per capita basis. Such a system of payment, it was claimed, would achieve a one-time reduc-

35. *Universal New York Health Care, UNY*Care*, Albany: New York State Department of Health, September 1, 1989. See also Dan E. Beauchamp and Ronald L. Rouse, "Universal New York Health Care: A Single-Payer Strategy Linking Cost Control and Universal Access," *New England Journal of Medicine*, September 6, 1990, pp. 640–44.

tion in administrative costs by establishing uniform payment rules and would enable additional long-run savings through fee limits.

UNY*Care would have limited private insurance liability to $25,000 annually. The state plan would cover annual costs above $25,000 for everyone and costs below that amount for anyone not covered by medicare or by employer-sponsored insurance. This cap on private liability would have narrowed variations in experience-rated premiums. It would have immediately given the state some leverage over costs because a relatively small number of very high-cost illnesses account for a large share of health care expenditures. Over time and if not adjusted for inflation, the cap would gradually shift responsibility for medical costs from private employer-sponsored insurance to a single state plan.

Governor Mario Cuomo embraced the plan in principle, but initially asked only for voluntary participation, promising full support later. The emergence of large budget deficits in the early 1990s made full support of the plan seem unlikely. Thus the New York plan was to begin as a voluntary incrementalist measure, move on to mandatory employer-sponsored insurance, and, if implemented along the lines of the 1989 proposal, become a single governmentally administered program.

THE CONSUMER-CHOICE HEALTH PLAN.   Alain Enthoven and Richard Kronick have proposed a health plan that includes mandatory employment-based insurance. It features regulatory measures to offset certain characteristics of free markets for health insurance and health care that make universal coverage impossible or needlessly expensive.[36] To deal with these problems, they propose the creation of

36. They write, "In a free market, health plans could pursue profits or survival by using numerous competitive strategies that would destroy efficiency and fairness and that individual consumers would be powerless to counteract: risk selection, market segmentation, product differentiation, discontinuities in coverage, refusals of insurance for some people, biased information, and anticompetitive behavior. Consumers avoid buying coverage until they get sick, and health plans protect themselves with elaborate strategies, including medical review (e.g., testing for the human immunodeficiency virus) and the exclusion of coverage for preexisting conditions." Alain C. Enthoven and Richard Kronick, "A Consumer-Choice Health Plan for the 1990s: Universal Health Insurance in a System Designed to Promote Quality and Economy," *New England Journal of Medicine*, January 5 and 12, 1989, pp. 29–37, 94–101 (quote on pp. 34–35).

financial agents or "sponsors" who would stand between employers and individuals, on the one hand, and providers of health care, on the other. The sponsors would regulate competition among health insurers and providers. For example, the sponsors would evaluate the expected medical outlays for various groups of people ("risk rating") and tag such groups with premiums that vary with risk, thereby reducing or eliminating the incentive of insurers to seek low-cost patients and reject high-cost patients. The sponsors would support studies to evaluate the quality and cost of various physicians and hospitals so that employers or individuals could buy services from relatively efficient providers. Enthoven and Kronick do not state clearly how these sponsors would be brought into existence, how many would operate in a given area, or whether they would be backed by government power.

The Enthoven-Kronick plan raises an issue that lies at the heart of private employment-based insurance: should insurance premiums vary with the risk characteristics or average health outlays of each group of employees? For reasons presented in chapter 2, and contrary to the position taken by Enthoven and Kronick, the answer in most cases seems to be no. If workplace risks or hazards vary by company, charging each company a premium that reflects these risks is economically efficient and seems just, because such a policy forces purchasers of that company's products to pay prices sufficient to cover these costs as well as other expenses of production. But variations in the cost of health care that are associated with the age, race, sex, disabilities, or health status of workers should not be allowed to affect relative prices of various commodities. Whatever the source, experience rating causes premiums for equivalent benefits to vary widely, with plans many times as costly for some companies as for others.[37] This line of argument raises the question of whether risk

---

37. Insurers for small businesses, which formerly charged universal rates, are increasingly charging the groups they cover different rates, "based on factors including occupation, location, and age and sometimes health of the members. . . . The rate for one group can be 5 times or even 15 times that of another group the same size. As one extreme example, a painting business in the Los Angeles area with three employees in their early 60's could pay more than $500 a person monthly, as against $50 a person for an accounting firm in Vermont with three employees in their 20's." Glenn Kramon, "Medical Insurers Vary Fees to Aid Healthier People," *New York Times*, March 24, 1991, p. 28. See also Stanley B. Jones, "Can Multiple Choice Be Managed to Constrain Health Care Costs?" *Health Affairs*, vol. 8 (Fall 1989), pp. 51–59.

rating, so essential for the operation of private insurance, is desirable in a national health plan, except possibly in special circumstances to help incorporate the costs of unsafe production into product prices. Experience rating raises issues entirely distinct from those concerning efforts of insurers to control risks through managed care and related methods.

The Special Problem of Long-Term Care

The development of private long-term-care insurance and the reform of public long-term-care protection are closely related and are shaped by three special characteristics of long-term care.

The first is the extreme concentration of long-term-care use among the very elderly, with the concomitant difficulty of persuading young people of the value of insurance against this remote contingency. However, once the risk is immediate and comprehensible, insurance costs more than most people can afford. As a result, private insurance companies have found it difficult to find a market for long-term-care insurance.

Second, although all health care includes some element of support for normal activities of daily living—shelter, eating, and toileting, for example—assistance with these activities is a larger component of long-term care than of acute care. Providing such services to the seriously disabled requires skill, training, and sensitivity, but these services are often provided by spouses, siblings, parents, other relatives, or friends. As a result, a much larger part of the cost of long-term care than of acute care goes for services most people provide for themselves or receive from others out of affection or duty and without charge. The provision of private or public long-term-care insurance therefore creates a larger risk of "moral hazard" than does acute-care insurance. For this reason, long-term-care benefits are payable only to potential beneficiaries certified to be incapable of performing one or more activities of daily living.

Third, most people who use long-term care do so only briefly. Three-quarters of all nursing home stays are less than one year. More than 80 percent of home care episodes for the community-based elderly last less than one year. But 56 percent of home care is provided to patients who receive care for three years or more.[38] For this reason and because insurers are concerned about moral hazard, the price of long-term-care insurance is acutely sensitive to the duration of home care or nursing home care for which potential beneficiaries must pay before they can claim insurance benefits.

These three characteristics of long-term care confront designers of insurance plans with some important choices. Alternative illustrative public benefits underscore the choices. A public plan that provided coverage as a matter of right, after a relatively brief deductible, for up to one year of long-term care would cover most long-term-care episodes. Private insurance would have to deal with only the minority of episodes lasting more than one year. Thus the social insurance program would serve as shallow coverage for everyone, leaving "catastrophic" episodes to private insurance or personal savings or, for the poor, to a means-tested benefit similar to that now provided under medicaid.

If the social insurance plan contained a large deductible but offered unlimited benefits after that deductible had been satisfied, the cost of short stays could be met from private insurance or savings, although some form of means-tested benefit would probably still be necessary for the poor. These two approaches differ in another key respect. The second plan would serve as "estate insurance" for the relatively wealthy, protecting potential heirs against the financial depredations of protracted incapacity. The first would provide no such protection, leaving to individuals the decision about how best to plan for heirs. The choice among these two and other approaches has implications for financing. Adoption of the second version would strengthen the case for increasing the estate and gift tax by lowering exemptions or increasing rates.

State Initiatives

State governments have taken steps to deal with rising costs and the incapacity or unwillingness of private insurers to cover many

38. Wiener and others, *Premium Pricing of Prototype Private Long-Term Care Insurance Policies,* table 11. This pattern resembles that of recipiency of unemployment insurance and welfare benefits. The pattern may depend in some degree on available arrangements of paying for long-term care. If the system of payment changed, the pattern of duration of care might well change.

small groups and some industries and occupations.[39] These efforts have taken a variety of forms. Massachusetts, as well as Hawaii, has enacted laws that require private employers to sponsor and pay for health insurance for most of their employees.[40] Various other states have moved to extend coverage gradually. The state of Washington created a state-supported program in 1987 to enable residents under age 65 to enroll in a health insurance plan, with subsidy for households with incomes less than twice official poverty thresholds; but appropriations permitted only about 3 percent of the uninsured to enroll. Minnesota enacted a program in 1987 to provide pregnancy and health services for children up to age 6 (raised in 1988 to age 8 and in 1991 to age 18) in families with incomes under 185 percent of official poverty thresholds who were not eligible for medicaid. Colorado, New Jersey, and New York have also enacted benefits for children, but a lack of money has slowed implementation.

Several states are trying to cut the price of health insurance for small groups. Rhode Island permits small companies that have not previously offered health insurance to sponsor plans with a reduced set of benefits. Kentucky has adopted similar rules. Connecticut has prohibited insurance companies from excluding particular individuals from insured groups and provided reinsurance to back up insurers who were prohibited from charging anyone more than 150 percent of standard premiums. Several states at various times have required those paying hospital bills to pay add-ons to reimburse hospitals for the costs of uncompensated care.

Oregon has pioneered with a proposal to rank all medical interventions under medicaid, increase the numbers of beneficiaries, and then use funds appropriated for medicaid to provide everyone covered by the program with as many services as possible, starting

39. For a review of state initiatives to control costs and extend insurance coverage, see Linda Demkovich, *The States and the Uninsured: Slowly but Surely, Filling the Gaps* (Washington: George Washington University, National Health Policy Forum, October 1990); and "1990 State by State Legislative Survey," *Federation of American Health Systems Review*, vol. 23 (September–October 1990), pp. 20–36.

40. The Massachusetts plan become law in 1988. It required companies to sponsor and pay for most of the cost of health insurance for most employees or pay a tax instead. The departure from office of the plan's sponsor, Democratic Governor Michael Dukakis, the succession of Republican William Weld, and the deterioration of the Massachusetts economy make full implementation of the plan unlikely. See Erik Eckholm, "Health Care Plan Falters in Massachusetts Slump," *New York Times*, April 11, 1991, p. A1.

from the most beneficial and moving down the list until funds are exhausted. Technical flaws led Oregon to withdraw its initial plan.[41] Colorado and Michigan considered the adoption of a similar plan. The practical question that any such plan must face is how to assure that limitations curtail relatively low-benefit care but not high-benefit care.

Nearly all the state initiatives promise to increase the numbers of people with financial access to health care. The crucial question for long-term reform is whether the efforts of the various states acting independently can achieve essentially universal health insurance coverage. The well-established role of the states as insurance regulators legitimates their efforts to prevent insurers from excluding some patients from group coverage and denying coverage for preexisting conditions. Even in Hawaii at least 5 percent of the population remains uninsured. No other state has moved as far as Hawaii, and the deterioration of the fiscal situation in many states makes it unlikely that they will do so. Although employer mandates do not directly increase state outlays, their full efficacy hinges on the extension of backup coverage, the cost of which requires state outlays for those outside the labor force and, possibly, subsidies to employers who cannot readily afford the mandate. The periodic financial crises to which states are subject puts them under strong pressure to curtail medicaid eligibility as well as benefit packages and reimbursement. States operating independently have only a modest capacity to extend insurance coverage significantly.

A 1990s Agenda for Health Care Financing

The U.S. health insurance system has done a respectable job of providing access to high-quality health care for the vast majority of Americans. But it has failed to provide coverage for more than 30 million people, to control rising costs, or to provide private financial protection against the expenses of long-term home care or nursing home care. Incremental reforms promise marginal improvements

41. "Oregon Reform Plan Delayed Again," *Medicine and Health*, vol. 44 (November 19, 1990), p. 1. For a critique of the Oregon plan, see William B. Schwartz and Henry J. Aaron, "The Achilles Heel of Health Care Rationing," *New York Times*, July 9, 1990, p. A17.

in each of these directions. Without significant changes in policy, however, prospects are slight that the U.S. system of paying for health care will do materially better during the 1990s than it has in the past, and it will probably do somewhat worse.

The U.S. system rests on three pillars: employer-financed health insurance voluntarily provided as a fringe benefit of employment; government-sponsored health insurance for the elderly and disabled, available as a right based on prior employment; and income- or means-tested benefits available to the poor. Under favorable gaze, the system is diverse and flexible; seen less charitably, it is fragmented and uncoordinated. Either way, American providers of health care receive income from more separate and independent payers than do providers in any other developed country.

Because so many separate groups pay for U.S. health care, providers have proven adept at resisting efforts to slow growth of spending. As cost consciousness has grown, each payer—public and private—has sought to make certain that it pays only for the costs generated by patients for whom it is responsible. Medicare payments have been reduced in a variety of ways—most notably through diagnosis related groups. Private companies have sought and received negotiated discounts from hospitals and physicians. Because the additional short-run cost of caring for one more patient typically is less than the average long-run cost of care, each payer can offer to pay providers (especially hospitals, which have large excess capacity) at rates that are attractive in the short run but devastating in the long run. As a result of such efforts, some hospitals, particularly those serving disproportionate numbers of the uninsured or medicaid recipients, are reporting deficits or sharply reduced profits.

As noted earlier, these efforts promise some savings by encouraging the elimination of purely wasteful expenditures. But they offer no effective barrier to continued medical cost increases caused by the proliferation of beneficial diagnostic and therapeutic interventions for patients who are well insured. Furthermore, as insurance companies charge each group or individual the full cost of expected medical outlays, the tendency increases for employers with above-average medical costs to limit or discontinue insurance plans, for employees faced with increased premiums or cost sharing to reject optional coverage, and for providers to reject uninsured patients.

In short, under the current payment system the effort to control health care costs is at war with the objective of extending coverage to the uninsured or even maintaining current coverage. Conversely, extension of insurance to the uninsured within the current framework would threaten increases in medical costs. Such a jump in costs could result from increasing pressure on available medical resources.[42] Extending insurance coverage would slightly boost real consumption of medical services, but the additional real costs would be less than proportional to the added numbers of people insured because the uninsured currently consume large quantities of medical care. According to one estimate, increasing the proportion of the American population with health insurance by 13.1 percent would directly increase health care spending by 4.6 percent.[43] Even a modest increase in the price of care for those already insured would sharply boost the total cost of extending coverage.

Thus a major challenge for health policy during the 1990s is to formulate strategies for extending health insurance coverage without fueling inflation of health care costs. To achieve both goals simultaneously will require some form of comprehensive restructuring, as outlined above. Voluntary incrementalism will not achieve a sufficient extension of insurance. Mandatory employer-sponsored insurance would not fundamentally alter the current system's payment structure, which prevents effective control of costs. The plans for comprehensive restructuring that retain employer-sponsored coverage would build on, rather than abandon, the enormous investment embodied in the current system of employer-sponsored health insurance. Each would mandate employer-sponsored coverage for all workers employed more than a minimum number of hours a week. But each also would lodge control over spending in powerful entities equipped to control physician reimbursement and to set hospital budget limits.

The obstacles to extending insurance against the costs of long-term care are, as noted, rather different from the problem of extending acute-care insurance. There is little prospect that those too

42. Hospital occupancy rates fell from an annual average of 77.1 percent in 1980 to 69.6 percent in 1989, signifying a considerable excess of beds nationally. Nevertheless, specific communities have high occupancy rates; and it is in these localities that inflationary pressures would be most pronounced.

43. *Cost and Effects of Extending Health Insurance Coverage*, Committee Print, pp. 73, 76, 81, 82.

poor to pay directly for long-term care but too rich to qualify for medicaid will be covered. Even if this judgment proves eventually to be unduly pessimistic, the prospect is slight that private insurance coverage for long-term care could match current coverage for acute care, and the chances that such a goal could be reached in this decade seem nonexistent.

The Universal-Access Single-Payer Health Plan

I propose a universal-access single-payer health plan that would provide acute and long-term health care insurance coverage for all U.S. residents and create a framework that can be used to limit the growth of spending. It rests on four propositions.

First, in common with most of the proposals for reform now under discussion, it presumes continuation of the system of employer-sponsored and -financed health insurance for working people and their families. Although a wholly public plan probably could achieve some additional administrative savings and some support persists for such an approach, the following plan is predicated on the unwillingness of Congress to shift the bulk of currently private health care outlays to public budgets and to displace current health care arrangements for most Americans.

Second, it presupposes that the current system can never provide coverage for people with little or no connection to the work force. The medicare system embodies such a presupposition for the elderly and disabled. The medicaid system reflects an understanding that employer-sponsored insurance will never serve more than a minority of the poor. The rest of the poor, as well as the unskilled and the long-term unemployed, can be assured access only through an extension of public coverage or through public payment for private insurance.

Third, in common with the proposals for fundamental restructuring, the plan described below posits that control over health care spending must be concentrated in one or a few hands. Efficient rationing of medical resources is more probable through some form of overall budget, rather than through controls on price per unit of service (such as the DRG system under medicare). Price limits provide no incentive to deny low-benefit care, but only avoid outlays for a given class of cases that consistently exceed some norm. A fixed budget permits physicians, hospital administrators, nurses, and other providers to implement rules for allocating limited resources to maximize medical benefits.

Fourth, the plan presented below is based on the presumption that federal action is necessary to set a floor under the provision of insurance coverage, but that in a country as large and diverse as the United States the allocation of health care spending and many elements of the design of health care benefits should be permitted to differ regionally. The federal government can use its regulatory powers, including tax rules, to achieve substantially universal coverage of working people and their families through private, employer-sponsored insurance for care during acute illness. And it will have to use its spending powers to assure coverage of people who cannot secure coverage through work. However, the case for encouraging regional variation is strong, particularly with respect to long-term care because of the large variations in costs and in the availability of home care, as well as the considerable current uncertainty about the best design for public support of long-term care.

Benefits and Plan Design

Because the system of paying for health care is likely to require major reform before the federal budget deficit has been eliminated, the plan sketched below is designed to help deal with both problems. Progress toward both goals can be achieved if reforms in the financing of health care are accompanied by measures to raise additional revenues at least sufficient to cover any added budgetary costs.

COVERAGE. The federal government would pursue a dual strategy. It would mandate that employers either sponsor coverage for all workers employed at least twenty-five hours a week and for their dependents and pay approximately three-fourths of the premium cost of this coverage, or pay a tax equal to roughly 9 percent of total payroll.[44] The requirement would apply to all employers, including the self-employed. The mandated coverage would include up to

44. This provision is taken from the plan of the National Leadership Commission on Health Care. The tax would apply whether or not particular employees were covered through another employer-sponsored plan of some relative.

120 days of hospitalization annually, unlimited physicians' services, specified preventive services (including maternity and prenatal care, routine examinations and unlimited care for preschool children, mammography, and Pap smears), inpatient and outpatient mental health benefits, and specified medications upon payment of a flat fee. All employers would be required to provide dependent coverage. Workers with low incomes would be entitled to a refundable personal income tax credit to prevent the net cost of coverage from exceeding roughly 5 percent of income. The federal government would also extend public coverage to people in families that have no one attached to the labor force and to employees of companies that elected to pay the tax instead of offering health insurance.

COST CONTROL. The federal government would establish general guidelines under which states, acting alone or jointly, would create a series of "financial agents" that would operate as the single payer for acute-care services in their areas. These agents, like those in the New York plan and unlike those in the Enthoven-Kronick plan, would be quasi-independent state regulatory agencies. Financial agents operating in standard metropolitan areas that span two or more states would be the responsibility of the states jointly; disputes among states would be settled by the federal government. Responsibility for administering limited budgets would rest with the financial agents. The financial agents would be empowered to establish and enforce payment schedules for physicians, such as the relative value scales used in medicare. They would negotiate hospital reimbursements and would be authorized to set fixed budgets as a means of controlling growth of hospital spending. They would be authorized to stipulate services that would be paid for only if rendered in hospitals and to specify which hospitals could receive payment for specified procedures. In this way, the financial agents could require the establishment of regional centers for the provision of particular services and prevent the proliferation of facilities outside the hospital setting. These powers are necessary to limit care to cases where benefits are judged sufficient to justify the costs. Without this power, entrepreneurial hospitals and physicians would continue to be reimbursed for investments in costly equipment for diagnosis or treatment, thereby making denial of low-benefit care difficult or impossible to enforce. In addition, the financial agents would be the conduit for federal payments to provide coverage for those not covered through employer-sponsored plans.

The federal government would set annual targets for the increase in total health care spending within financial agents' areas. These overall spending targets would set the limits on total spending, but the financial agents would determine how that total should be distributed among various medical services.

The financial agents would not supplant private insurers. Private insurers would cease to make payments to providers, but they would continue to market insurance to businesses. Initially, premiums for acute-care coverage would continue to be experience rated. But each financial agent would have responsibility for designing a gradual transition to a form of community rating that complied with broad and loosely drawn federal guidelines. Financial agents would be allowed to retain rate differences demonstrably related to workplace hazards or personal habits such as smoking or consumption of alcohol or other drugs. Rate variations based on workers' personal characteristics, such as age, race, sex, or disability status, would be prohibited. The financial agents could permit some local variation in the number and definition of groups. The transition from experience rating to community rates would have to be complete within five years of adoption of the plan. Companies that do not now sponsor health insurance and that would experience large proportionate increases in costs would be eligible for federally funded subsidies until the transition to community rating was complete.

PRIVATE "STOP-LOSS" PROTECTION. To strengthen the hand of the financial agents in cost control and to ease the transition to community rating, an annual limit on liabilities of private insurers should be set along the lines proposed in the New York state plan. In that way, the financial agents would be responsible for high-cost episodes of care. But the principal initial insurance responsibility of the financial agents would be to pay for acute health care for people not covered under employer-sponsored insurance, along the lines proposed by the National Leadership Commission on Health Care and other proposals to mandate workplace coverage.

The stop-loss limit would be the focus of debate on whether the United States is to retain a mixture of employer-sponsored and public insurance or will shift gradually to all-public financing, with the gradual elimination of private companies from the health insurance business.[45] If the stop-loss limit were raised as fast as medical costs, private insurers would retain a secure position in the system of paying for health care costs for most people. If the stop-loss limit were frozen, inflation would gradually lower the size of the market covered by private insurers until the remaining market was too small to support continued operations.

LONG-TERM CARE.   The financial agents would also serve as the channel for financing long-term home care and nursing home care. Their role would depend on a national decision about the nature of the public role in supporting long-term care.

At least three broad courses of action are open. First, the nation might try to encourage the purchase of private health insurance through a variety of tax concessions and perhaps some direct subsidies. Unless the subsidies are quite large, many or most of the elderly who come to require long-term care will be uninsured. This course of action would require a large income- or means-tested public program for the support of long-term care. The financial agents would be the natural managers of this program. Because many financial agents would exist throughout the United States, they could retain much of the discretion now enjoyed by the states in regulating vendors of home care and nursing homes. Standards of eligibility should be established nationally, rather than locally, however, to reduce the existing wide national disparities in access to care.

Adoption of a national social insurance program is the second option for supporting long-term care. A social insurance program could provide home health services or nursing home care as a matter of right to those suffering from stipulated limitations on activities of daily living.[46] As noted earlier, a social insurance program can take many forms. Under some versions, a large income- or means-tested backup program would remain essential. The financial agents should administer any such backup program and should assume state regu-

45. Some major insurance companies, including Aetna and Teachers Insurance and Annuity Association, have elected to withdraw from the health insurance market in some or all states.

46. For illustrative plans, see Ball, *Because We're All in This Together*; and Alice M. Rivlin and Joshua M. Wiener with Raymond J. Hanley and Denise A. Spence, *Caring for the Disabled Elderly: Who Will Pay?* (Brookings, 1988).

latory functions concerning vendors of home care and nursing homes.

The third option neither institutes a new social insurance program nor relies on private insurance to provide access to long-term care. Rather, it entails grants from the federal government to state or local governments or nonprofit organizations operating under limited budgets to underwrite home care and nursing home services up to the limits of available funds. This approach could provide the same services for given total expenditures as the other options, but it would reduce the risk inherent in the social or private insurance approaches—that demand, supported by a financial entitlement, would result in much larger than anticipated costs. A new long-term-care entitlement could face such a cost "surprise" if unexpectedly large numbers of the disabled elected to use benefits to which they had become newly entitled. The grant mechanism would also create an instrument, absent from the social insurance approach, for controlling costs of providers.

Reorganization of Federal Health Care Activities

The new federal health program would assume most current health activities of the federal government, including medicare, which could be retained in its current form or folded into the larger system of paying for acute care. Medicaid would become part of the backup program for those not covered under employer-sponsored plans. Most Veterans Administration facilities should be put under the aegis of the financial agents except for special missions of this organization (treatment of spinal cord injuries, for example) that might not be adequately served in a unified framework. The federal employees health benefits program and CHAMPUS would be treated like other employer-sponsored plans and required to channel financing through the financial agents.[47] Outlays for these activities under current policy are projected to reach $205 billion in 1991 (table 5-1). But the universal-access single-payer health plan would have additional responsibilities. It would direct subsidies to the private companies required to offer health insurance that face particularly high

47. In general, the goal would be to vest a single agency with responsibility for all health care activities classified under budget accounts 551 and 553. Health research would remain a federal responsibility.

Table 5–1. *Proposed Health Care Trust Fund, 1991*
Billions of 1991 dollars

Expenditures		Revenues	
Current activities		*Current earmarked revenues and state payments*	
Medicaid	79	Payroll tax and medicare trust fund interest	87
Medicare	104	Contribution to medicare Part B	12
Veterans' health	13		
Other	9	State medicaid outlays (estimated)	34
Subtotal	205	Subtotal	133
Additional activities[a]		*Additional revenues*[a]	
Acute care	40	Employer payments in lieu of insurance	30
Long-term care	25	Tax on employer-financed health insurance above cap	9
		Value-added tax at 6 percent[b]	102
Total	270	Total	274
Addendum: Reduction in federal deficit relative to current policy			
Added revenue	141		
Added expenditure	65		
Deficit reduction	76		

Sources: *Budget of the United States Government, Fiscal Year 1992*, pp. 4-9, 7-55, 7-58; and *Overview of Entitlement Programs, 1990 Green Book, Background Material and Data on Programs Within the Jurisdiction of the Committee on Ways and Means: 1990 Edition*, Committee Print, House Committee on Ways and Means, 101 Cong. 2 sess. (Government Printing Office, 1990), pp. 162, 1290. Figures are rounded.

a. Author's estimates.

b. Based on Congressional Budget Office, *Reducing the Deficit: Spending and Revenue Options*, February 1990, pp. 144, 417–20, assuming full effectiveness by 1991. The VAT revenues assume the CBO "narrow base" plus medical expenditures. The inflationary effects of the VAT on medical prices are assumed to be offset by cost control measures.

costs. And it would finance the new long-term-care program. Total expenditures in 1991 would be an estimated $270 billion if the programs were all fully in effect.

The total budget of the federal health care agency that administers the universal-access single-payer health plan would exceed the current budget of all federal departments, other than the Department of Defense and the Social Security Administration. Under plausible projections, health care outlays under current policy will exceed defense outlays late in the 1990s and social security benefits after about 2009.[48] Because expenditures on health care are large and

48. *Budget of the United States Government, Fiscal Year 1991.* These crossovers would occur sooner if responsibilities for the health department were increased or if defense or social security outlays fell below projections.

certain to keep growing, it would be sound budgetary procedure to house these functions in an independent cabinet-level Department of Health and to finance federal expenditures on health care through a trust fund, like those now used for social security pensions and medicare hospital benefits.

Financing

The activities of the new Department of Health would be financed through three main sources (see table 5-1). The first and most important would be revenues currently collected to pay for medicare and funds allocated by states to medicaid;[49] and premiums now paid by individuals for part B medicare coverage ($133 billion). The second would be payments by employers who elected to pay taxes rather than sponsor insurance (approximately $30 billion) and revenues from a cap placed on the value of employer-financed insurance that employees can exclude from personal income tax ($9 billion). The cap on excludable premiums is assumed to be $100 a month for individuals and $250 a month for families. The third source would consist of new tax revenues earmarked for the finance of health care. An earmarked value-added tax of 6 percent would yield approximately $102 billion. As an alternative revenue source, an increase in the payroll tax from its current level of 15.3 percent of covered earnings to 19.3 percent would yield approximately $100 billion. Doubling federal tobacco taxes and imposing a tax of $0.25 per ounce of ethyl alcohol in beverages would yield about $10 billion a year.[50] Repealing the 1981 increase in the exemption used in calculating federal estate and gift taxes and adjusting the prior exemption for inflation would yield $1 billion, an increase which can be easily justified on the grounds that long-term-care benefits would protect estates against the devastation wrought by chronic disabling illnesses.

49. Federal legislation would be necessary to ensure that states did not reduce their outlays.

50. Whether alcohol or tobacco consumption creates financial burdens for people other than the consumers is not clear. Consumption of alcohol and tobacco increases the frequency of many illnesses, but it also shortens life expectancy, thereby reducing the incidence of other illnesses and lowering pension costs. On this issue, see Thomas C. Schelling, "Economics and Cigarettes," *Preventive Medicine*, vol. 15 (September 1986), pp. 549–60.

The additional taxes would cover added federal expenditures on acute and long-term care and also reduce the overall deficit. Because federal expenditures now financed out of general revenues would be shifted to the health trust fund, this plan would reduce the federal deficit by approximately $76 billion. The increase in taxes would be determined by the target for deficit reduction and the health care benefits—especially the range of acute-care benefits mandated under the acute-care plan and the extent of patient cost sharing; the terms of long-term-care benefits, including notably whether these benefits are financed through a new social insurance program or through grants to states, localities, and selected providers; and the size of transitional subsidies offered to employers forced to sponsor acute-care insurance.

The Federal Role: Short and Long Run

The role of the federal government as direct provider and manager of health insurance would be smaller under the universal-access single-payer health plan than under current law. Administration of health care plans would reside with state or regional bodies—the financial agents—rather than with federal agencies. But the federal government would have greatly expanded financial responsibility for raising revenues sufficient to support costs of acute-care health benefits for those not covered through work, high-outlay episodes of acute care for everyone, and long-term care. It would establish the budget constraints within which the financial agents would have to operate.

Criticisms

Major reforms of important institutions are always subject to criticism. The universal-access single-payer health plan is no exception. Like any other fundamental reform, the universal-access single-payer health plan will redistribute responsibility for financing health care, generating costs and savings in a somewhat capricious manner. Businesses that do not sponsor health insurance will be forced to do so and incur the associated costs. Eventually these costs may be offset by slowed growth in money wages or other fringes, but some businesses will suffer some competitive disadvantages in the meantime. On the other hand, companies that now sponsor plans may find their costs reduced, as providers' costs for uncompensated care decline. And taxes will go up to pay for services formerly paid by private payers and new services. Some citizens will gain and some will lose.

The answer to this criticism is that the only way to avoid such redistribution is to continue the current system, a course that I have argued is not open. Therefore the only issue concerns the pattern and amount of redistribution. The universal-access single-payer health plan would cause less redistribution than would other major alternatives, including large refundable tax credits (a centerpiece of the voluntary incrementalist strategy) or vouchers funded from tax revenues. In any event, the choice among reforms should not be driven solely by such transitional problems but should be made by weighing them against improvements in access and in the capacity to control costs.

Other criticisms of the universal-access single-payer health plan hold that it is not really necessary, because less disruptive reforms that do not impinge on free choice by businesses and individuals could ensure access and enable cost control. I have argued above that this view is hard to accept because private actions are unlikely to control the provision of low-benefit, high-cost care or assure access to all. Even if the strategy of voluntary incrementalism were eventually to work, it would take many years, during which millions would still be unable to afford care and expenditures on low-benefit, high-cost care would continue.

The most serious criticisms of the universal-access single-payer health plan concern the workability of its specific elements: mandated employer-sponsored insurance and the financial agents. The administrative problems associated with mandatory employer-sponsored insurance are real.[51] To prevent gaps in coverage, rules will be necessary to stipulate whether workers who are between jobs are covered by their old employer or the public backup plan. Some employers will undoubtedly supplement any mandated benefit package. Two-worker families will have to decide under which plan to

51. Some criticisms relate to mandates that retain experience rating and are not applicable to the universal-access single-payer health plan. Katherine Swartz, "Why Requiring Employers to Provide Health Insurance Is a Bad Idea," *Journal of Health Politics, Policy, and Law*, vol. 15 (Winter 1990), pp. 779–92.

include their children. Workers who change jobs will experience changes in their coverage. These complexities are costly and inconvenient, but they are the price of building on, rather than replacing, the current system. If the United States were designing its health care financing system from scratch, I do not think that it would choose to base it on employer-sponsored insurance. But the investment in the current system is huge. The task of reformers should be to find politically acceptable ways to improve the current system, not to argue what might be the best system if current arrangements did not exist.

Economists point out that mandating employer sponsorship and financing of health insurance is equivalent to an increase in the minimum wage and therefore threatens the jobs of some workers, especially those earning roughly the minimum wage.[52] The jobs of teenagers have been shown to be more vulnerable to increases in the minimum wage than those of mature workers. Teenagers are more likely to be working part time and hence not to be subject to an employer mandate. But the cost of some lost jobs is real. That is one of the reasons I have urged that employers should be offered the option of paying a modest tax in place of covering the costs of health insurance or that transitional subsidies should be offered to employers who would experience large increases in costs.

Another potential difficulty with the universal-access single-payer health plan is the uncertain capacity of the financial agents to make rational allocational decisions. The existence of federally imposed spending limits will require such choices if Congress uses its authority to keep the growth of spending low enough to require the denial of some beneficial care to some people. The success of the financial agents in making rational allocational decisions will depend on the progress of effectiveness research. Even more important will be the development of procedures and criteria for deciding which services provide benefits too small to justify their costs. These techniques do not yet exist. The attempt by Oregon to develop such procedures illustrates the importance and the difficulty of finding analytically and politically defensible policies.

52. Standard theory suggests that mandated health insurance will tend to cause money wages or other fringe benefits to fall. Such adjustments cannot take place for workers receiving the minimum wage or a bit more. Swartz, "Why Requiring Employers to Provide Health Insurance Is a Bad Idea," p. 788.

A Time to Begin

In brief, the universal-access single-payer health plan would provide essentially universal financial access to acute care. It would greatly expand access to long-term care. And by creating budget-constrained entities that are empowered to negotiate fees and hospital budgets, it would establish the basis for control over the growth of medical care costs. Whether this power would be used to hold down costs would hinge on national support for budget limits. That such support would be forthcoming is not assured, but other countries in which a larger part of health care spending is under governmental control have been more successful than the United States in restraining growth of health care spending.

The universal-access single-payer health plan would not automatically assure high-quality care or lead to improved information about the efficacy of various medical interventions. The achievement of this goal under any system of paying for health care hinges on continuation and expansion of publicly sponsored effectiveness research.

This plan would leave open how the U.S. health care system should evolve. If the dollar limit used to cap the liability of employer-sponsored health plans for acute care were raised annually by the rate at which health care spending rose, private insurance companies would retain a major role in the provision of employment-based insurance. Insurance companies could continue to compete for sales on the basis of service, quality monitoring, and benefits in addition to those required under law, but not on the basis of premiums, which would be set by community rating. While such competition would be attenuated by the standardization of price, it would retain some of the incentive for innovation that distinguishes the current system. The price of such competition would be a continuation of the extra selling costs and other administrative expenses associated with multiple insurers.

Alternatively, if the limit on liability of employer-sponsored plans were not adjusted for inflation, the role of private health insurance in financing acute health care would gradually shrink and eventually vanish. Although revenues of insurance companies from this source would decline, any adjustments would take place over many years and would be easily managed both for companies and employees.

The financial agents would come to finance health care entirely with revenues from public sources.

In short, the United States can achieve universal health insurance coverage now and can immediately strengthen the capacity of the system to combat rising costs, while leaving for later debate the divisive question of what role private insurance should ultimately play. Access to health care for the uninsured and control of health care costs for everyone should not be held hostage to divisions over the ultimate goals for an ideal system.

Index